MISS JANE AUSTEN'S GUIDE
TO MODERN LIFE'S DILEMMAS

MISS JANE AUSTEN'S GUIDE TO MODERN LIFE'S DILEMMAS

Answers To Your Most Burning Questions
About Life, Love, Happiness (and What To Wear)
from the Great Novelist Herself

REBECCA SMITH

JEREMY P. TARCHER / PENGUIN
a member of Penguin Group (USA) Inc.
New York

I will always maintain the importance of aunts. This is for my very dear aunts and great aunts.

*"Follies and nonsense,
whims and inconsistencies,
do divert me,
I own, and I laugh at them
whenever I can."*

ELIZABETH BENNET IN
PRIDE AND PREJUDICE

JEREMY P. TARCHER/PENGUIN
Published by the Penguin Group
Penguin Group (USA) Inc.,
375 Hudson Street,
New York 10014, USA
Penguin Group (Canada)
90 Eglinton Avenue East, Suite 700,
Toronto ON M4P 2Y3, Canada
(a division of Pearson Penguin Canada Inc.)

Penguin Books Ltd
80 Strand, London,
WC2R 0RL, England

Penguin Ireland
25 St Stephen's Green,
Dublin 2, Ireland
(a division of Penguin Books Ltd)

Penguin Group (Australia)
250 Camberwell Road,
Camberwell,
Victoria 3124, Australia
(a division of Pearson Australia Group)

Penguin Books India Pvt Ltd
11 Community Centre,
Panchsheel Park,
New Delhi – 110 017, India

Penguin Group (NZ)
67 Apollo Drive, Rosedale,
North Shore 0632, New Zealand
(a division of Pearson New Zealand Ltd)

Penguin Books (South Africa) (Pty) Ltd
24 Sturdee Avenue, Rosebank,
Johannesburg 2196, South Africa
Penguin Books Ltd, Registered Offices:
80 Strand, London,
WC2R 0RL, England

This edition published by
Penguin Group (USA) Inc., 2010

Published simultaneously in Canada

Most Tarcher/Penguin books are available at special
discounts for bulk purchase for sales promotions,
premiums, fund-raising, and educational needs.
For details, write to Penguin Group (USA) Inc. Special
Markets, 375 Hudson Street, New York, NY 10014.

Library of Congress Cataloging-in-Publication data is
available on request

Color origination by Ivy Press Reprographics

Printed in China
10 9 8 7 6 5 4 3 2 1

ISBN: 978-0-39916-061-5

This book was conceived, designed, and produced by
Ivy Press
210 High Street, Lewes
East Sussex BN7 2NS, UK
www.ivypress.co.uk

CREATIVE DIRECTOR Peter Bridgewater
PUBLISHER Jason Hook
ART DIRECTOR Wayne Blades
SENIOR EDITOR Jayne Ansell
DESIGNER Glyn Bridgewater
PICTURE MANAGER Katie Greenwood

CONTENTS

LOVE & RELATIONSHIPS

IS HE THE ONE? SHOULD I MAKE A MOVE? WILL
HE CHANGE? DO AGE GAPS MATTER? SOUND
FAMILIAR? JUST SOME OF THE MANY PERENNIAL
DILEMMAS SUFFERED IN THE NAME OF LOVE
AND RELATIONSHIPS. NOT MUCH HAS
CHANGED SINCE JANE AUSTEN'S DAY (WELL,
APART FROM THE HATS AND DANCE STEPS),
SO WHY NOT LET HER WIT, WISDOM, AND
CHARACTERS HELP YOU SORT OUT
YOUR LOVE LIFE?

CAN A MAN REALLY CHANGE?

Q YOU KNOW THAT NO ONE IS PERFECT AND THAT ANY MAN, NO MATTER HOW WONDERFUL, COULD DO WITH SOME IMPROVEMENT. YOU WOULDN'T MIND SO MUCH IF THE FLAWS REMAINED HIDDEN FROM VIEW, BUT THE SAD FACT IS, YOUR BOYFRIEND EMBARRASSES YOU IN PUBLIC. THE OBNOXIOUS WAY HE SHOVELS FOOD INTO HIS MOUTH, THE RUDE COMMENTS, AND THE SLIGHTLY INAPPROPRIATE PUBLIC DISPLAYS OF AFFECTION MEAN YOU CRINGE WHEN HE UTTERS THE WORDS "LET'S EAT OUT TONIGHT." IS HE A LOST CAUSE OR COULD HE LEARN TO BEHAVE?

> *Mr. Rushworth was an inferior young man, as ignorant in business as in books, with opinions in general unfixed, and without seeming much aware of it himself ... indifference was the most favorable state they could be in. Her behavior to Mr. Rushworth was careless and cold. She could not, did not like him.*
>
> MANSFIELD PARK

 Your boyfriend isn't a lost cause, but your relationship might be. There will be somebody out there to appreciate him for what he is, but that person isn't you. If he makes you cringe now, how will you react in a few months or years? Of course nobody's perfect, and even Mr. Darcy needed improvement before Lizzy Bennet could marry him, but if your boyfriend makes you cringe, he shouldn't be your boyfriend. If it were just one little thing, you could ask him to alter it, but your troubles are clearly more serious.

How would you sum up your boyfriend? When Jane Austen falls for Tom Lefroy she writes to her sister Cassandra that he is a "very gentleman-like, good-looking, pleasant young man." * Could you say that of your boyfriend? Jane says that Tom "has but one fault, which time will, I trust, entirely remove—it is that his morning coat is a great deal too light." She may not like his choice of coat, but he, like her, is a great reader and dancer. It could be love.

Perhaps the most touching lines of any of Jane's surviving letters are these, written the day before a ball, when she thinks that Tom will propose: "I look forward with great impatience to it, as I rather expect to receive an offer from my friend in the course of the evening. I shall refuse him, however, unless he promises to give away his white coat." †

One suspects that even the light-color coat could have been livable if finances had made the match acceptable to their families, but the couple had no money and the proposal was never made.

Jane would advise you to ask yourself some questions and listen to your good sense and your heart. Why are you with your boyfriend? Is it because you just want a boyfriend, any boyfriend? Could it be his money? This is the catastrophic mistake that Maria Bertram makes in *Mansfield Park*. Maria realizes that Mr. Rushwood is stupid and annoying, but she is tempted by his money and she doesn't want to be left on the shelf. She avoids him and is embarrassed by him. Sound familiar? If you notice the noise a man makes when he's eating, you are not in love. Are you bothered by a coat in the wrong color or something more fundamental? Act accordingly.

* Letter to Cassandra, Steventon, January 9th, 1796. † Letter to Cassandra, Steventon, January 14th, 1796

WHY AM I STILL SO INTIMIDATED BY THE BARBIES OF THE WORLD?

 IT SEEMS THAT YOU'RE SURROUNDED BY IMAGES OF UNREALISTICALLY BEAUTIFUL WOMEN—GLOSSY MAGAZINES FULL OF PHOTOSHOPPED STARS AND MUSIC VIDEOS PARADING SUPERTONED BODS ARE DOING THEIR PART TO SAP YOUR CONFIDENCE. YOU KNOW THAT KIND OF PERFECTION IS IMPOSSIBLE, BUT DEEP DOWN YOU CAN'T HELP BUT MEASURE YOURSELF AGAINST IT ... AND YOU'RE AFRAID THAT EVERYBODY ELSE JUDGES YOU THAT WAY, TOO. HOW CAN YOU STOP WORRYING AND LEARN TO LOVE YOURSELF FOR WHO YOU ARE?

 Stop consuming so much trash and start reading books and watching shows that will make you happier. These perfect women don't exist—they really don't. You must stop thinking of yourself as inferior and start living as the heroine of your own life. You don't need to start out looking like Barbie to have a happy ending. Consider Catherine Morland: "No one who had ever seen Catherine Morland in her infancy would have supposed her born to be an heroine ... the Morlands [...] were in general very plain, and Catherine, for many years of her life, as plain as any. She had a thin awkward figure, a sallow skin without color, dark lank hair, and strong features ..." *

Catherine will never become a particularly accomplished young lady: indeed she doesn't care much for "improving" herself: "The day which dismissed the music-master was one of the happiest of Catherine's life" and she "loved nothing so well in the world as rolling down the green slope at the back of the house."†

* *NA*, Ch1. † Ibid.

Catherine becomes slightly less plain as she gets older, and eventually can be described as "almost pretty." When she goes to stay in Bath, her life takes off. She has plenty to learn, but because she is open and friendly, people want to be with her.

Lizzy Bennet isn't an obvious heroine either. When Mr. Darcy first sees her, he doesn't think she's pretty: "But no sooner had he made it clear to himself and his friends that she had hardly a good feature in her face, than he began to find it was rendered uncommonly intelligent by the beautiful expression of her dark eyes."* Jane loved Elizabeth. In January 1813, the year of the novel's publication, she wrote: "I must confess that *I* think her as delightful a creature as ever appeared in print, and how I shall be able to tolerate those who do not like *her* at least I do not know." †

Millions of readers do love her. It doesn't matter if you start out as rather plain, but if you consume trash you will feel trashy. Throw away the magazines, stop watching pop videos, and read more novels. You'll soon feel much better.

Jane describes the best sort of reading matter:

"And what are you reading, Miss——?"

"Oh! It is only a novel!" replies the young lady, while she lays down her book with affected indifference, or momentary shame. "It is only Cecilia, *or* Camilla, *or* Belinda; *or, in short, only some work in which the greatest powers of the mind are displayed, in which the most thorough knowledge of human nature, the happiest delineation of its varieties, the liveliest effusions of wit and humor, are conveyed to the world in the best-chosen language."*

NORTHANGER ABBEY

---

* *P&P*, Ch6. † Letter to Cassandra, Chawton, January 29th, 1813

HOW CAN I STOP BEING A SHRINKING VIOLET?

 YOU HATE STANDING OUT FROM THE CROWD. YOU CAN'T EVEN WEAR HIGH HEELS TO WORK WITHOUT WONDERING IF PEOPLE WILL THINK YOU'RE RIDICULOUS, BUT NOW THERE'S A MAN IN YOUR OFFICE WHO YOU REALLY LIKE. HE ALWAYS STOPS TO CHAT WHEN HE PASSES YOUR DESK AND SAVES YOU A CHAIR AT MEETINGS. YOU'VE FINALLY PLUCKED UP ENOUGH COURAGE TO ASK HIM OUT, BUT YOU'RE WORRIED ABOUT THE AFTERMATH IN YOUR GOSSIPY OFFICE. THE LAST THING YOU WANT IS TO BECOME THE LATEST WATER-COOLER SENSATION AND DRAW ATTENTION TO YOURSELF. HOW CAN YOU LET HIM KNOW YOUR FEELINGS AND STILL KEEP THINGS ON THE DOWN LOW?

He likes you—that is clear. He wants to sit next to you and it sounds as though he's just as nice as you are, so unless he's also chatting up other women in the office, you can bet he's interested in you, too. With your natural reserve, you won't come across as pushy, as long as you don't feel compelled to act out of character; but you are in danger of losing him if he doesn't start to realize how you feel. If you want the friendship to blossom into something more, you must tell him that you are Actually Interested.

Jane Bennet is a paragon of niceness, but she almost loses the chance to marry Mr. Bingley, a man with whom she is in love, because she is too discreet to let her feelings show. Mr. Darcy explains how it seems in a letter to Elizabeth: "... From that moment I observed my friend's behavior attentively; and I could then perceive that his partiality for Miss Bennet was beyond what I had ever witnessed in him. Your sister I also watched. Her look and manners were open, cheerful, and engaging as ever, but without any symptom of peculiar regard, and I remained convinced from the evening's scrutiny, that though she received his attentions with pleasure, she did not invite them by any participation of sentiment ..." *

You must make sure you show some symptoms of "peculiar regard" for this man. Buy him a cup of coffee and a muffin to go with it. This is not being too forward, and you won't make yourself look ridiculous. Ask him to help you with something. If you start being even more nice and friendly (but only to him), you may find that he does the actual asking out. Because Mr. Bingley is a shy fellow and not terribly confident either, he's easily persuaded that Jane doesn't love him. Don't let the same thing happen to your possible Mr. Right.

Take a leaf out of Catherine Morland's book. She's not the kind of girl who'd wear a plunging neckline, but because she lets Henry Tilney know that she likes him by responding to all of his overtures without being pushy, she gets to live happily ever after. You must try to be a little less Jane Bennet and a little more Catherine Morland.

> "It may perhaps be pleasant," replied Charlotte, "to be able to impose on the public in such a case; but it is sometimes a disadvantage to be so very guarded. If a woman conceals her affection with the same skill from the object of it, she may lose the opportunity of fixing him; and it will then be but poor consolation to believe the world equally in the dark ..."
>
> PRIDE AND PREJUDICE

* *P&P,* Ch25

AM I TOO YOUNG TO BE TIED DOWN?

Q YOU'RE IN YOUR EARLY TWENTIES AND BLISSFULLY HAPPY IN YOUR RELATIONSHIP. IN FACT, YOU'VE NEVER FELT SO LOVED. CLEARLY YOUR BOYFRIEND FEELS THE SAME WAY, BECAUSE HE'S ASKED YOU TO SPEND THE REST OF YOUR LIFE WITH HIM. WHILE YOU'D BE HAPPY IF YOU SAID YES, AND YOU DEFINITELY DON'T WANT TO LOSE HIM, YOU REALIZE YOU'RE STILL YOUNG AND THERE'S A LOT OUT THERE YOU HAVEN'T EXPERIENCED YET. PART OF YOU IS WORRIED THAT YOU'LL NEVER KNOW WHAT IT'S LIKE TO BE YOUR OWN PERSON. SHOULD YOU TIE THE KNOT OR SEVER THE TETHER AND SPEND TIME FINDING YOURSELF?

> *"I lay it down as a general rule, Harriet, that if a woman doubts as to whether she should accept a man or not, she certainly ought to refuse him. If she can hesitate as to 'Yes,' she ought to say 'No' directly. It is not a state to be safely entered into with doubtful feelings, with half a heart. I thought it my duty as a friend, and older than yourself, to say thus much to you. But do not imagine that I want to influence you."*
>
> EMMA

 Emma Woodhouse might be pushing her friend in the wrong direction, but her actual advice is good. If there are doubts in your heart about accepting this lovely man now, you should refuse him, but (and I feel like underlining this) only say that you cannot marry him right away.

The method you use to turn him down must be carefully chosen. You might regret it if you break things off completely, and even if another Mr. Wonderful comes along, you'll spend the rest of your life wondering "what if?" Jane Austen was a counselor to her niece, Fanny Knight. Fanny (whose mother had passed away) confided in her Aunt Jane when it came to affairs of the heart. Jane loved her dearly, telling her: "You are inimitable, irresistible. You are the delight of my life."*

Jane did her best to advise her, but was concerned about persuading her niece in the wrong direction, and letters show her swinging between being for and against the young man under consideration. Perhaps Jane was thinking of this when she started work on *Persuasion*; she was aware that what she said to Fanny might have life-changing consequences: "... as to opinion or counsel," Jane wrote in 1814, "I am sure that none will be extracted worth having from this letter." †

But people have been quoting that letter (and others) for generations now. Jane's advice is sound: "... nothing can be compared to the misery of being bound *without* love—bound to one, and preferring another; *that* is a punishment which you do *not* deserve." ‡

Both Jane and her characters give this advice: do not say "yes" until you are sure. Even if it is Mr. Darcy doing the asking, you should reserve your "yes" until you have no doubts.

---

* Letter to Fanny Knight, Chawton, February 20th, 1817. † Letter to Fanny Knight, Chawton, November 18th, 1814.
‡ Letter to Fanny Knight, London, November 30th, 1814

One of Jane's concerns was that Fanny hadn't yet seen enough of life and met enough young men to know if this suitor was the one for her—perhaps you are in the same situation: "Poor dear Mr. J. P.! Oh, dear Fanny! Your mistake has been one that thousands of women fall into. He was the *first* young man who attached himself to you. That was the charm, and most powerful it is."*

And: "When I consider how few young men you have yet seen much of; how capable you are (yes, I do still think you *very* capable) of being really in love; and how full of temptation the next six or seven years of your life will probably be (it is the very period of life for the *strongest* attachments to be formed). I cannot wish you with your present very cool feelings to devote yourself in honour to him." †

* Letter to Fanny Knight, Chawton, November 18th, 1814. † Letter to Fanny Knight, London, November 30th, 1814

Beware of saying yes to this man just because he is the first to become important to you. If he really loves you, he will let you put the question on hold. If he won't, it might tell you that underneath he could be a bully. Mr. Darcy asked Lizzy Bennet again. Captain Wentworth (eventually) asked Anne Elliot again. Colonel Brandon bided his time until he knew Marianne Dashwood was ready for the question.

You must very gently explain that you just aren't ready to give your "yes" yet, that you want to spend longer learning about life together (stress the "together") and that you want to get married once you've done all this. This should buy you enough time to decide.

All this said, be careful! You must not make the mistake Anne Elliot first made—don't break it off entirely or you may lose him forever. It takes years for Captain Wentworth to get over his wounded pride.

> *"My dear, dear Lizzy, I would—I do congratulate you; but ... are you quite certain that you can be happy with him? ... And do you really love him quite well enough? Oh, Lizzy! do anything rather than marry without affection. Are you quite sure that you feel what you ought to do?"*
>
> *"Oh, yes! ..."*
>
> PRIDE AND PREJUDICE

Jane's advice would be that you must not listen to anybody else's advice—only that of your own heart: "... you must not let anything depend on my opinion; your own feelings, and none but your own, should determine such an important point ... I dare not say, 'Determine to accept him'; the risk is too great for *you*, unless your own sentiments prompt it." *

The second time Robert Martin asks Harriet Smith to marry him, she says yes right away. She doesn't need to ask Emma, and is sure that her answer is the right one. I expect there's somebody somewhere writing a novel called *Harriet* ...

* Letter to Fanny Knight, London, November 30th, 1814

HOW DO I TURN A HINT INTO A SLEDGEHAMMER?

Q A WEEK AGO YOU MET A GUY WHILE OUT WITH YOUR GIRLFRIENDS. YOU WEREN'T THAT ATTRACTED TO HIM BUT HE SEEMED NICE; SO, WHEN HE ASKED, YOU GAVE HIM YOUR NUMBER. IT TURNS OUT HE'S AN AMATEUR STALKER— YOU'VE BEEN BOMBARDED WITH TEXTS AND PHONE CALLS FROM HIM ASKING YOU OUT EVERY DAY SINCE YOU MET HIM, AND HE'S EVEN TRACKED YOU DOWN ON FACEBOOK. YOU'VE TRIED TO BE NICE AND LET HIM DOWN GENTLY, BUT HE'S NOT GETTING THE MESSAGE AND NOW YOU'RE ANNOYED. HOW CAN YOU MAKE IT CLEAR YOU'RE NOT INTERESTED?

A He seemed nice, so are you really sure that he isn't? What made you give him your number? Were you just being friendly, or were you intoxicated, perhaps as much by the atmosphere of the evening as by whatever you had imbibed? What kind of heroine do you want to be? Are you a Lydia Bennet, still thinking of dancing with other officers as she packs to elope with Wickham? Consider this response: "'Pray make my excuses to Pratt for not keeping my engagement, and dancing with him to-night. Tell him I hope he will excuse me when he knows all; and tell him I will dance with him at the next ball we meet, with great pleasure.'" *

Or do you want to be an Elizabeth Bennet or an Emma Woodhouse, who learns from her experiences? This man may have seemed nice but you have made a mistake. By giving him your number, you have also given him the message you're interested in getting to know him.

* *P&P*, Ch47

Carry on being polite, but not too friendly. Lizzy has to do this in declining Mr. Collins (her cousin and a guest in her house) but she would never have given him her number. When she first tells him "no" he doesn't believe her, so she has to tell him more emphatically.

Leave it as long as possible before replying to the texts or calls, and then try saying something neutral about the weather. Emma tries this strategy when Mr. Elton has her cornered. If that doesn't work, you must make your position very clear. First apologize for giving him the wrong impression, and then tell him politely that you are not interested and that you only meant to be friendly. This is exactly Emma's situation with Mr. Elton. She has been unwittingly leading him on and should have read the signs better.

If this man still isn't willing to accept your apology, you must do what Lizzy and Emma eventually find necessary— resort to silence.

Mr. Collins only finally accepts Lizzy's "no" when it comes via her father. If this man is a true stalker, you, too, will have to ask somebody to intervene on your behalf.

> *"Upon my word, sir," cried Elizabeth, "your hope is rather an extraordinary one after my declaration. I do assure you that I am not one of those young ladies (if such young ladies there are) who are so daring as to risk their happiness on the chance of being asked a second time. I am perfectly serious in my refusal. You could not make me happy, and I am convinced that I am the last woman in the world who would make you so …"*
>
> PRIDE AND PREJUDICE

You may have been behaving at the Lydia Bennet end of the spectrum, but unless you want to end up with a Wickham or a Mr. Elton on your hands, you should think before giving out your number.

WHAT COUNTS AS CHEATING ON YOUR BOYFRIEND?

YOU'RE TWO MONTHS INTO A NEW RELATIONSHIP AND IT'S THE LONGEST YOU'VE EVER HAD. YOU'RE A NATURALLY CHATTY AND FLIRTY WOMAN—YOU ENJOY GETTING TO KNOW NEW PEOPLE—BUT YOU'RE WONDERING IF YOUR USUAL FLIRTY BEHAVIOR MIGHT BE A STEP TOO FAR. THIS IS NEW TERRITORY FOR YOU AND YOU'D RATHER NOT SCREW UP YOUR BUDDING ROMANCE. SO, IS FLIRTING THE SAME AS CHEATING, OR IS IT OKAY AS LONG AS YOU DON'T TAKE IT ANY FURTHER?

Your boyfriend has fallen for you, so he must appreciate your vivacity, and unless he has a personality disorder, he won't want to stop you from talking to people, but you must start to tread more carefully.

Jane Austen loved to chat and dance and flirt. There is an oft-quoted contemporary description of Jane, that she was the "prettiest, silliest, most affected husband-hunting butterfly ever"; * but this opinion was formed by somebody who didn't know her very well, and whose family was involved in a hugely significant lawsuit against Jane's brother, Edward.

Many people think that Mary Crawford is the real heroine of *Mansfield Park*; she's witty, pretty, and fun to be with, she looks beautiful when she plays the harp, but she makes shockingly rude jokes. Sadly, her inability to rein herself in costs her dearly. If she had taken her cues from Edmund Bertram and changed her behavior, she might have found happiness with him. She cuts a sad figure the last time we see her, draped around a door frame, trying to lure him back: "'I had gone a few steps,

---

*The author, Mary Russell Mitford, wrote in a letter to Sir William Elford in 1815 that this was how her mother remembered the young Jane Austen. Mary was actually a fan of Jane's work. These letters are quoted in Austen-Leigh, W. and Austen-Leigh, R., *Jane Austen – A Family Record*, revised by Le Faye, D. (1989).

> *In Lydia's imagination, a visit to Brighton comprised every possibility of earthly happiness. She saw, with the creative eye of fancy, the streets of that gay bathing place covered with officers. She saw herself the object of attention to tens and to scores of them at present unknown. She saw all the glories of the camp—its tents stretched forth in beauteous uniformity of lines, crowded with the young and the gay, and dazzling with scarlet; and, to complete the view, she saw herself seated beneath a tent, tenderly flirting with at least six officers at once.*

PRIDE AND PREJUDICE

Fanny, when I heard the door open behind me. "Mr. Bertram," said she. I looked back. "Mr. Bertram," said she, with a smile; but it was a smile ill-suited to the conversation that had passed, a saucy playful smile, seeming to invite in order to subdue me; at least it appeared so to me. I resisted; it was the impulse of the moment to resist, and still walked on.'" *

Try to place yourself on the mousy / chatty / flirty scale. At one end, we have Fanny Price, and at the other, those incorrigible flirts, Henry Crawford and Lydia Bennet. Balanced in the middle but well on the side of fun is Elizabeth Bennet. She should be your model, so chat away, but don't go too far. Elizabeth carries on being her delightful self, but everyone will know to whom her heart belongs.

* *MP*, Ch47

23

HOW CAN I SHARE MY LIFE WITH MY FIANCÉ BUT NOT MY MONEY?

Q YOU SPENT YEARS MANAGING YOUR OWN FINANCES BEFORE YOU MET YOUR FUTURE HUSBAND, AND' YOU DID A PRETTY GOOD JOB, IF YOU DO SAY SO YOURSELF. YOU CERTAINLY DON'T BELIEVE MARRIAGE MARKS THE END OF INDEPENDENCE. NOW YOUR FIANCÉ WANTS TO SET UP A JOINT BANK ACCOUNT. YOU'RE NOT SO EAGER, AND WOULD PREFER TO KEEP THINGS SEPARATE. HOW DO YOU NAVIGATE THESE TRICKY FINANCIAL WATERS WITHOUT SINKING THE MATRIMONIAL SHIP?

A Jane knew the pleasure to be had in the successful management of one's own finances. She kept neat annual accounts, and although she loved shopping, she didn't waste money. Until Jane started earning as a novelist, she was entirely dependent on her family. How she must have gloried in the arrival of those publisher's checks. Her accounts show her making gifts and spending money on those she loved as well as on necessities. One of the last things she did before leaving Chawton for the final time was make a will, leaving almost all of her money (just over £531) to Cassandra and £50 each to Henry and his housekeeper, Madame de Bigeon. *

Her bequests speak volumes: Henry was broke, and he'd been the one to act for her (as convention demanded) in her dealings with publishers. Madame de Bigeon had lost money when his bank collapsed. This must have weighed on Jane's heart—a woman of little fortune was not to be impoverished by the Austens.

---

* According to The National Archives Currency Converter, £531 in 1817 would be equivalent to around £20,000 today, or roughly $30,000, and £50 to around £2,000, or $3,000, but changes in purchasing power and relative property values make exact comparisons difficult.

She was also trying to give Cassandra a future that was more Miss Woodhouse (secure) than Miss Bates (precarious). "The rich are always respectable," she had written to Cassandra on June 29th, 1808, a sentiment that is expanded upon in one of Emma's many edifying little lectures to Harriet Smith.

Elinor Dashwood and Anne Elliot both had the financial management skills to steer their families through choppy waters. Heroines must be capable of balancing the books and economizing, and they must be able to give presents to those they want to.

I Jane Austen of the Parish of Chawton do by this my last will & testament give and bequeath to my dearest sister. Cassandra Elizabeth everything of which I may die possessed, or which may be hereafter due to me, subject to the payment of my Funeral expences, & to a Legacy of £50. to my Brother Henry, & £50 to Mde de Bigeon— which I request may be paid as soon as convenient. And I appoint my said dear Sister the executrix of this my last will & testament.

JANE AUSTEN, APRIL 27TH, 1817
TRANSCRIPT OF JANE AUSTEN'S WILL FROM THE NATIONAL ARCHIVES

We'll assume that you are marrying Mr. Knightley, or at the very least dependable Robert Martin, but just in case your fiancé turns out to be a Wickham or a Willoughby with a trail of debts, or somebody with a serious shopping habit like Robert Ferrars, keep your wits about you. Jane would never have wanted to give up control of her finances, and nor should you. Yes, have a joint account for all that you share and do together, but keep a separate one for yourself, too.

HOW DO I REASON WITH A MAN
WHO REFUSES TO DANCE?

YOU JUST LOVE TO DANCE. IT'S BEEN THIS WAY EVER SINCE YOU WERE LITTLE: THERE'S SOMETHING ABOUT FEELING YOUR BODY IN MOTION THAT MAKES YOU BLISSFULLY HAPPY. YOU'VE TAKEN A FEW DANCE CLASSES ON YOUR OWN AND PARTNERED UP WITH STRANGERS, BUT NOW THAT YOU HAVE A BOYFRIEND YOU'VE BEEN EYEING A LOCAL SALSA CLUB THAT OFFERS COUPLES' CLASSES. UNFORTNUATELY, YOUR MAN IS LESS THAN ENTHUSED. HE SAYS DANCING IS FOR GIRLS. HOW CAN YOU LURE HIM INTO THOSE DANCING SHOES?

Jane Austen loved to dance. Her heroines love to dance—even Fanny Price likes dancing. In Jane's day, dancing afforded women the freedom to chat and flirt, to see and be seen, to exercise and have some fun. But not all Jane's heroes are eager to dance. Everybody remembers Mr. Darcy's reluctance. Sir William Lucas tries to persuade him:

"'… What a charming amusement for young people this is, Mr. Darcy! There is nothing like dancing after all. I consider it as one of the first refinements of polished societies.'
'Certainly, sir; and it has the advantage also of being in vogue among the less polished societies of the world. Every savage can dance.'" *

However, we shouldn't judge too hastily; sometimes those who are the most eager to dance aren't the good guys.

* *P&P*, Ch6

> *It may be possible to do without dancing entirely. Instances have been known of young people passing many, many months successively, without being at any ball of any description, and no material injury accrue either to body or mind;—but when a beginning is made—when the felicities of rapid motion have once been, though slightly, felt—it must be a very heavy set that does not ask for more.*
>
> EMMA

Frank Churchill loves dancing, and he and Emma Woodhouse get very excited about planning a ball. He's nice to dance with, but he isn't to be trusted. Mr. Knightley is actually a good dancer, but he's a bit jealous of Frank and rather scornful of the young people's plans: "'Very well. If the Westons think it worth while to be at all this trouble for a few hours of noisy entertainment, I have nothing to say against it, but that they shall not choose pleasures for me. Oh! yes, I must be there; I could not refuse; and I will keep as much awake as I can; but I would rather be at home, looking over William Larkins's week's account …'"*

Listen to Mr. Knightley. You should not choose pleasures for people either. Although he's disgruntled by the appearance of Frank on the Highbury scene, he doesn't behave with bad grace. He's kind enough to dance with Harriet Smith when she needs a partner, and because he loves Emma and wants her to be happy.

Perhaps your boyfriend is shy and worried about his lack of prowess on the dance floor. You should be sensitive to this, and do what Jane and her siblings would have done—practice at home. Kindness is more important than the ability to salsa. If you cannot gently persuade your boyfriend to dance, don't make him.

E, Ch30

HOW CAN I AVOID BECOMING A BRIDEZILLA?

Q YOU'RE OF AN AGE NOW WHEN YOU AND ALL YOUR ACQUAINTANCES SEEM TO BE GETTING HITCHED, BUT THAT'S NOT THE PROBLEM. THESE DAYS IT SEEMS TO BE AN UNSPOKEN RULE THAT THE AMOUNT OF MONEY YOU SPEND ON YOUR WEDDING EQUATES WITH HOW MUCH YOU AND YOUR PARTNER LOVE EACH OTHER, AS IF THE MARRIAGE IS FATED TO DISSOLVE AFTER FIVE YEARS MAXIMUM IF YOU DON'T RENT ELEPHANTS. YOU'D PREFER TO HAVE A LOW-KEY AFFAIR AND SAVE YOUR MONEY FOR A DOWN PAYMENT ON A HOUSE, BUT THE SNIDE COMMENTS ARE MAKING YOU WORRIED THAT YOU'RE SENDING THE WRONG MESSAGE. DO MOST PEOPLE REALLY THINK THIS WAY?

A All too often, when people decide to get married, the wedding is seen as being the important thing. A momentous decision is subsumed by thoughts of seating assignments and place settings. But what is important is not the wedding but the marriage; only somebody silly will be more concerned about one day and its finery than the marriage and its consequences.

Consider Mrs. Bennet when the letter arrives telling her that Lydia and Wickham are going to be married: "'My dear, dear Lydia!' she cried: 'This is delightful indeed!—She will be married!—I shall see her again!—She will be married at sixteen! ... But the clothes, the wedding clothes! I will write to my sister Gardiner about them directly. Lizzy, my dear, run down to your father, and ask him how much he will give her ... the things should be ordered immediately.' She was then proceeding to all the particulars of calico, muslin and cambric ..."*

* *P&P*, Ch49

Poor Mrs. Bennet—she truly cares about her daughters' futures, but here she is forgetting the financial ruin and ostracism that Lydia and Wickham have almost brought upon them all. Mr. Bennet (although having done nothing himself to prevent the calamity) is firm, and his wife learns to her "amazement and horror, that her husband would not advance a guinea to buy clothes for his daughter. He protested that she should receive from him no mark of affection whatever on the occasion."*

Do you really need to have a fancy wedding in order to be happily united? The most important thing is that you and your fiancé share ideals and, as you say, truly love each other. Jane Austen didn't waste words describing the weddings of Elizabeth and Jane Bennet—her pen dwells instead on how happy their marriages were. What is the wedding of Emma Woodhouse and Mr. Knightley like? They could have afforded to splurge but chose not to. Mrs. Elton thought it was a very poor show, but you shouldn't care what the Mrs. Eltons of the world think.

However wedding-obsessed those around you are, and however provoking their comments, just smile, keep quiet and remember that you are like Emma marrying Mr. Knightley. While your silly acquaintances will still be paying for their weddings, you will be happily married in your very own Donwell Abbey or Hartfield.

Mrs. Elton, from the particulars detailed by her husband, thought it all extremely shabby, and very inferior to her own … "Very little white satin, very few lace veils; a most pitiful business! … Selina would stare when she heard of it." … But, in spite of these deficiencies, the wishes, the hopes, the confidence, the predictions of the small band of true friends who witnessed the ceremony, were fully answered in the perfect happiness of the union.

EMMA

* *P&P*, Ch50

SHOULD I DATE AN OLDER GUY?

 HE'S KIND, HE'S GORGEOUS, HE'S RELIABLE, AND HE TREATS YOU LIKE A LADY. HE'S ASKED YOU OUT AND YOU'VE SAID YES. SO WHAT'S THE PROBLEM? WELL, IT'S JUST THAT HE'S TWENTY YEARS YOUR SENIOR. YOU HAVE NO PROBLEM WITH THE AGE DIFFERENCE, BUT YOUR FRIENDS THINK IT'S WRONG FOR YOU TO DATE A GUY WHO'S NEARER YOUR DAD'S AGE THAN YOUR OWN. SHOULD YOU LISTEN TO YOUR FRIENDS OR FOLLOW YOUR HEART?

Perhaps your friends are just jealous; perhaps they are wishing that he had noticed them, and if he really is gorgeous, kind, and reliable, who can blame them? But because you are at the "just-going-out-on-a-date" stage, you shouldn't be running ahead of yourself anyway. As Mr. Darcy himself puts it: "'A lady's imagination is very rapid; it jumps from admiration to love, from love to matrimony, in a moment ...'"*

So just enjoy your date for what it is, and don't let your thoughts run away with you. Of course, it is important

> *Colonel Brandon ... was silent and grave. His appearance, however, was not unpleasing, in spite of his being in the opinion of Marianne and Margaret an absolute old bachelor, for he was on the wrong side of five-and-thirty; but though his face was not handsome his countenance was sensible, and his address was particularly gentleman-like.*
>
> SENSE AND SENSIBILITY

* *P&P*, Ch6

that you don't trifle with each other, so if you think there is a real stumbling block to the relationship going anywhere, you should cool things off very quickly.

When Marianne Dashwood first meets Colonel Brandon, she doesn't consider him a prospect at all, saying that, "thirty-five has nothing to do with matrimony." She and Margaret (her little sister) dismiss him as being practically an old man: "'But he talked of flannel waistcoats,' said Marianne; 'and with me a flannel waistcoat is invariably connected with the aches, cramps, rheumatisms, and every species of ailment that can afflict the old and the feeble.'" *

Marianne didn't have the advantage of seeing Colonel Brandon being played by Alan Rickman in the 1995 movie of *Sense and Sensibility*, or she would have seen his potential sooner; but after a couple of years and much suffering at the hands of the far younger Willoughby, she finds true happiness with the man she once dismissed as being almost decrepit: "Marianne could never love by halves; and her whole heart became, in time, as much devoted to her husband, as it had once been to Willoughby." †

I think that the subtly emphasized "in time" is particularly interesting. Marianne gets her happy ending; but is Jane Austen saying that it is a qualified one? Some readers have found Marianne's destiny disappointing and unsatisfactory. But Jane tells us that Willoughby deeply regretted losing Marianne, not that she regretted losing him. Marianne finds fulfillment and happiness. Perhaps Jane is reminding us that we might not see how wonderful somebody is right away.

If Marianne's story isn't enough to convince you to keep an open mind about age gaps, consider the case of Emma Woodhouse. The opening line tells us that Emma is not quite twenty-one. The first thing we learn about Mr. Knightley is that he is about seventeen years older than that, but he proves to be a far better bet than the puppyish Frank Churchill.

CAN A LONG DISTANCE RELATIONSHIP WORK?

Q YOU'VE BEEN WITH YOUR BOYFRIEND FOR A WHILE AND YOU LOVE EACH OTHER VERY MUCH. BUT NOW HIS JOB IS TAKING HIM OUT OF THE COUNTRY FOR AT LEAST TWO YEARS. IT'S AN AMAZING OPPORTUNITY AND YOU SUPPORT HIM WHOLEHEARTEDLY; YOU'RE JUST NOT SURE YOU SUPPORT THE IDEA OF A ROMANCE AT A DISTANCE. YOU COULDN'T POSSIBLY JOIN HIM FOR AT LEAST A YEAR. IS IT BEST TO BREAK UP NOW AND SAVE THE HEARTACHE OR TOUGH IT OUT FOR LOVE?

A "'There is nothing so bad as a separation,'" says Mrs. Musgrove in *Persuasion*,* but, of course, there *is* something worse: losing the one you love forever. Cassandra Austen could tell you about this. In 1792, she became engaged to Tom Fowle, a former pupil of her father's school. There was a problem, however—the usual one—not enough money for them to settle down. Tom became a clergyman, and in 1796 he went as a chaplain to the West Indies. The idea was that once he had earned enough money, they would be able to marry,

* *P*, Ch8

but Tom contracted yellow fever and died. Cassandra was heartbroken and never fell in love again. Should she have ended the engagement before he went? Of course not—they knew the risks before he set sail, but thought it better to love and hope and look to the future.

Anne Elliot does what seems sensible. She is in love with Frederick Wentworth but is persuaded against entering into a long engagement. This decision brings years of unhappiness: "Her attachment and regrets ... for a long time, clouded every enjoyment of youth; and an early loss of bloom and spirits had been their lasting effect."*

> *"Ah!" cried Captain Harville, in a tone of strong feeling, "if I could but make you comprehend what a man suffers when he takes a last look at his wife and children, and watches the boat that he has sent them off in, as long as it is in sight, and then turns away and says, 'God knows whether we ever meet again!' And then, if I could convey to you the glow of his soul when he does ..."*
>
> PERSUASION

Anne gets another chance with her love, but you might not. Perhaps you could plan to be like Mrs. Croft, who decides that the only thing to do is to be with her husband as often as she can: "'In the fifteen years of my marriage,' she says, 'I have crossed the Atlantic four times, and have been once to the East Indies ... besides being in different places about home: Cork, and Lisbon, and Gibraltar ...'" †

Perhaps you think that you would be being kind by ending things now; well, that's another mistake Anne Elliot makes. Poor Captain Wentworth is so devastated that it takes him years to pluck up the courage to try to get her back. Your boyfriend probably won't die from yellow fever, and you have Skype and e-mail, so unless you are looking for a reason to break things off, try to tough this out.

* *P*, Ch4. † *P*, Ch8

MY BOYFRIEND KEEPS BUYING ME THINGS I HATE. HOW DO I STEER HIM IN THE RIGHT DIRECTION?

Q YOUR NEW MAN IS AN INCURABLE ROMANTIC. HE PRESENTS YOU WITH TOKENS OF HIS AFFECTION AT EVERY OPPORTUNITY, WHICH YOU CAN HARDLY COMPLAIN ABOUT, EXCEPT ... WELL, IN THIS CASE YOU CAN, BECAUSE HE KEEPS BUYING YOU THE MOST AWFUL, USELESS THINGS. WHILE YOU KNOW IT'S THE THOUGHT THAT COUNTS, IT'S FRUSTRATING THAT HE DOESN'T PUT A LITTLE MORE CARE INTO WHAT HE'S BUYING YOU. IS THERE A GOOD WAY TO PASS ON THE HINT THAT THE GIFTS ARE UNNECESSARY OR, EVEN BETTER, TO POINT HIM TOWARD THE THINGS YOU LIKE?

... for upon trial the one given her by Miss Crawford would by no means go through the ring of the cross. She had, to oblige Edmund, resolved to wear it; but it was too large for the purpose. His, therefore, must be worn; and having, with delightful feelings, joined the chain and the cross— those memorials of the two most beloved of her heart, those dearest tokens so formed for each other by everything real and imaginary— and put them round her neck, and seen and felt how full of William and Edmund they were, she was able, without an effort, to resolve on wearing Miss Crawford's necklace, too.

MANSFIELD PARK

This is a tricky one. As the recipient of a gift you should, of course, act in a grateful way, but I wonder if these gifts are demonstrating that the two of you just aren't very well suited. It's time to look at the relationship as a whole and consider how compatible you really are. Are they jokey little things? Perhaps you just don't share his sense of humor. Or are they more considered purchases? Perhaps he is putting a lot of thought into them, but you have completely the wrong idea of each other. Just as he may not be right for you, you may not be right for him. On the other hand, could it be that you are just a horrible and ungrateful person and he'd be better off with somebody else?

Willoughby shows what a thoughtless and impulsive person he is when he tries to give Marianne Dashwood a horse. Poor Marianne—she must be missing her lovely old home and its beautiful grounds—but in their newly straitened circumstances, the Dashwoods couldn't possibly afford to keep a horse and employ

the help necessary to look after it. Better not to be offered a horse than to have to say "no, thank you." It takes Elinor to point out that the present isn't well considered. She ventures "to doubt the propriety of her [Marianne] receiving such a present from a man so little, or at least so lately known to her."* It is only when Elinor points out the sacrifices that their mother would have to make to pay for it all, that Marianne sees sense. A person can be simultaneously extravagant and thoughtless.

* S&S, Ch12

35

Jane Fairfax receives a surprise gift in *Emma*, and although she must have been pleased to be given a beautiful piano, the speculation and embarrassment it causes are a different matter. Imagine the scene when a piano turns up unannounced at her aunt's tiny apartments.

Mr. Knightley puts it plainly and sensibly: "'But they would have done better had they given her notice of it. Surprises are foolish things. The pleasure is not enhanced, and the inconvenience is often considerable.'" *

Fanny Price is given a most beautiful and welcome surprise in *Mansfield Park*. Carefully chosen by her brother William, it is "the almost solitary ornament in her possession, a very pretty amber cross" from Sicily. † Jane and Cassandra Austen received topaz crosses (also welcome surprises) from their own sailor brother, Charles. Jane clearly loved hers and so it makes a cameo appearance in her work.

William Price can't yet afford a chain to go with the cross and poor Fanny is thrown into terrible confusion when she thinks she'll have to choose between

> *Marianne told her, with the greatest delight, that Willoughby had given her a horse, one that he had bred himself on his estate in Somersetshire, and which was exactly calculated to carry a woman … She had accepted the present without hesitation, and told her sister of it in raptures. "He intends to send his groom into Somersetshire immediately for it," she added, "and when it arrives, we will ride every day. You shall share its use with me. Imagine to yourself, my dear Elinor, the delight of a gallop on some of these downs."*
>
> SENSE AND SENSIBILITY

* *E*, Ch26. † *MP*, Ch26

*"Oh, this is beautiful indeed! This is the very thing, precisely what
I wished for! This is the only ornament I have ever had a desire to possess.
It will exactly suit my cross. They must and shall be worn together.
It comes, too, in such an acceptable moment. Oh, cousin, you do not
know how acceptable it is."*

MANSFIELD PARK

wearing one that Mary Crawford gives her (a necklace that seems to come with
strings attached) and one from her beloved cousin, Edmund. In the end, the
Crawford one is too big to fit through the cross's tiny loop, so she is able to use
the one she wants to and wear the other as an extra necklace. Edmund's is the right
one—he and she are meant to be together—he is a person who can choose a
perfect present for her. Of course, Fanny doesn't love her brother any less because
he can't afford a gold chain to go with the cross. She does, however, feel all the
extra weight that comes with the Crawford gift.

Be as sensible as Elinor and ask him (as politely as Fanny Price would) to please
refrain from giving you any more surprises, then see what happens. Meanwhile,
you should think about what it is that you and your boyfriend really want to give
to and accept from each other.

HOW DO I INTRODUCE A NEW MAN TO MY SOMEWHAT CRAZY FAMILY?

Q YOU'VE BEEN DATING THIS NEW SQUEEZE FOR A WHILE NOW, AND YOU THINK HE MIGHT BE A KEEPER. OF COURSE, NOTHING'S EVER CERTAIN IN LOVE OR WAR, SO YOU'RE STILL A LITTLE HESITANT ABOUT TAKING HIM HOME TO MEET YOUR MOM AND DAD AND THE REST OF YOUR LARGE AND, SOME WOULD SAY, INTIMIDATING CLAN. SHOULD YOU JUMP IN AT THE DEEP END AND INVITE HIM TO THE FAMILY REUNION PICNIC, OR INTRODUCE HIM TO ONE FAMILY MEMBER AT A TIME?

What you need here is an ally. When Elizabeth Bennet becomes engaged (at last!) to Mr. Darcy, she worries about her family's reaction. She wants to protect her beloved and at the same time let them know what a wonderful person he is. If her Aunt and Uncle Gardiner had been nearby, they would have helped her; they were trusted by everybody and already knew what an altogether good thing Mr. Darcy was, having spent time with him in Derbyshire and London.

Going for a grand announcement is definitely not the easiest or smoothest way to do things. Follow clever Lizzy's example, and start by introducing him and the idea of the two of you as an item to somebody in the family you can trust, then tell a few key players and let the news spread before the big picnic.

Elizabeth starts by confiding in her sister Jane, and she soon has somebody on her side. Remember that it is better to let important individuals know about your beloved in advance instead of springing him on them at a big occasion. Nobody likes to feel that they've been kept in the dark.

Mr. Darcy asks Lizzy's father for permission to marry her (as tradition dictated) and Lizzy reassures him that Mr. Darcy really is The One. It's notable that Lizzy (instead of her father or sister) is the one to tell Mrs. Bennet. Lizzy wants to make sure that she has her mother somewhere quiet and alone. Do the telling yourself— you may need to reassure people or give them the chance to get used to the idea in private: "When her mother went up to her dressing room at night she followed her, and made the important communication. Its effect was most extraordinary; for, on first hearing it, Mrs. Bennet sat quite still, and unable to utter a syllable." *

> *She anticipated what would be felt in the family when her situation became known; she was aware that no one liked him but Jane, and even feared that with the others it was a dislike which not all his fortune and consequence might do away. At night she opened her heart to Jane.*
>
> PRIDE AND PREJUDICE

You may find that you're pleasantly surprised by your relatives' reactions. Lizzy dreaded how her mother would behave toward Mr. Darcy, but: "... the morrow passed off much better than she expected; for Mrs. Bennet luckily stood in such awe of her intended son-in-law that she ventured not to speak to him, unless it was in her power to offer him any attention, or mark her deference for his opinion." †

People will be pleased to see you happy, and there will be plenty of other things for people to think about when you are all outdoors. Jane would also advise some skillful preparation to smooth the way. She knew that food is a great distraction. "Strawberries, and only strawberries, could now be thought or spoken of." ‡

* *P&P*, Ch59. † Ibid. ‡ *E*, Ch42

DO DIFFERING MUSICAL TASTES MEAN
A FLAT NOTE IN OUR RELATIONSHIP?

 YOU'VE ALWAYS BEEN A MODERN GIRL—YOU LOVE YOUR UP-TO-THE-MOMENT INDIE BANDS. BUT YOUR NEW MAN IS RETRO ALL THE WAY—HE'S ARDENT ABOUT HIS JAZZ CLUBS. THE RELATIONSHIP IS STILL NEW, BUT YOU'RE WORRIED THAT YOUR POLAR-OPPOSITE MUSIC TASTES SPELL IMMINENT DOOM FOR THE TWO OF YOU. DO YOU REALLY NEED TO MARCH TO THE BEAT OF THE SAME DRUMMER TO MAKE THINGS WORK?

> *"I could not be happy with a man whose taste did not in every point coincide with my own. He must enter into all my feelings; the same books, the same music must charm us both ... the more I know of the world, the more am I convinced that I shall never see a man whom I can really love. I require so much!"*
>
> SENSE AND SENSIBILITY

When Marianne Dashwood makes this impassioned little speech, she is reminded by her mother that she is only seventeen and has a bit more to learn about life. Then onto the scene comes Willoughby. Marianne has sprained her ankle, and he literally sweeps her off her feet and carries her home. In a society where men and women rarely touched each other, to be picked up and held like this would have been almost overwhelming. It seems the most romantic way to begin and: "They speedily discovered that their enjoyment of dancing and music was mutual, and that it arose from a general conformity of judgment in all that related to either ... Their taste was strikingly alike. The same books, the same passages were idolized by each ..." *

So far so good—or so it seems—but Elinor is already suspicious: "'Well, Marianne,' said Elinor, as soon as he had left them, 'for <u>one</u> morning I think you have done pretty well. You have already ascertained Mr. Willoughby's opinion in almost every matter of importance ... You know what he thinks of Cowper and Scott ... You will soon have exhausted each favorite topic. Another meeting will suffice to explain his sentiments on picturesque beauty, and second marriages, and then you can have nothing farther to ask.'" †

Willoughby's untrustworthy nature is gradually revealed. Poor Marianne— he looked like a storybook hero and seemed to share her passions, so she fell for him. But there was a real hero on the scene before Willoughby. Colonel Brandon listened with respect while Marianne played the piano and sang.

After Willoughby has dumped Marianne, Colonel Brandon is there through her long convalescence, and she discovers that there is a wonderful world of things yet to be enjoyed: "'I know the summer will pass happily away ... Our own library is too well known to me, to be resorted to for anything beyond mere amusement. But there are many works well worth reading, at the Park; and there are others of more modern production which I know I can borrow of Colonel Brandon ...'" ‡

Don't worry that you and your man have differing tastes in music. Jane knew that learning about each other's likes and dislikes is part of the fun. A future with Colonel Brandon and his library is one worth looking forward to.

* *S&S*, Ch10. † Ibid. ‡ *S&S*, Ch46

WHAT SHOULD I BE LOOKING FOR IN A MAN?

 MANY GIRLS DREAM OF BRAVE, HANDSOME, CASTLE-OWNING KNIGHTS IN SHINING ARMOR WHO SWOOP DOWN TO RESCUE THEM FROM DRAGONS, DRUDGERY, OR DOLDRUMS. AS YOU GET OLDER, HOWEVER, YOU REALIZE THAT NO PACKAGE IS PERFECT OR COMPLETE, AND THAT SOMETIMES YOU HAVE TO CHOOSE SOME TRAITS AT THE EXPENSE OF OTHERS. YOU WANT LOVE BUT VALUE FINANCIAL STABILITY; YOU ALSO WANT TO BE ATTRACTED TO HIS BODY AS MUCH AS HIS MIND. SO IS IT BETTER TO SEARCH FOR A MATE WITH MORE PRACTICAL TRAITS, OR SHOULD YOU THROW CAUTION TO THE WIND AND DATE THE POOR BUT HUNKY LIFEGUARD?

And now, my dear Fanny, having written so much on one side of the question, I shall turn round and entreat you not to commit yourself farther, and not to think of accepting him unless you really do like him. Anything is to be preferred or endured rather than marrying without affection ...

LETTER TO FANNY KNIGHT, LONDON, NOVEMBER 18TH, 1814

 Jane Austen's emphatic advice to her niece on this issue would have made a perfect opening line. We see the consequences of marriages entered into for the wrong reasons again and again in Jane's novels; just think of the unhappy situations of the Bennets, the Palmers, and the Prices. The principle is clear—do not marry without affection, you will live to regret it.

This advice might seem obvious to us now, but choices for women in Jane's time were so limited that even an offer of marriage from some odious toady like Mr. Collins would have merited consideration. For Jane or one of her heroines, the answer would always be "no," but the alternative might well be a life of poverty and dependence on the charity of one's relatives. When Jane decided not to accept Harris Bigg-Wither, the awkward younger brother of her life-long friends Alethea and Catherine Bigg, she was turning down financial security for herself and her mother and sister. She wouldn't have accepted a man unless she loved him and thought that they were truly compatible and that he was her intellectual equal.

One of the first signs we have that Frank Churchill is not all that he seems is when he goes to London for the day and says it is to get his hair cut: "'Hum!' says Mr. Knightley, 'just the trifling, silly fellow I took him for.'" * Frank's on a secret mission, but allowing himself to appear that vain shows some serious deficiency, a deficiency that Mr. Woodhouse, for all his gentle ways, senses, too.

Date the poor but hunky lifeguard if he'll have you, but don't expect to be happy forever unless you have plenty to talk about. If a relationship is based on lust, happiness won't last. Maria Bertram and Henry Crawford end up thoroughly sick of one another, and Lizzy Bennet despairs of Wickham and Lydia's future together: "How little of permanent happiness could belong to a couple who were only brought together because their passions were stronger than their virtue." †

Jane would never "give her hand without her heart," ‡ but none of her heroines give their hearts unless their heads are in agreement, too. There are no happy endings without good sense as well as love, and none of the heroines end up without financial security. The Austen happy ending required the full package, and Jane chose to forgo marriage because it seemed that she couldn't have that. You'll know when the right man comes along. If it feels like a compromise, it's wrong.

* *E*, Ch25. † *P&P*, Ch50. ‡ *MP*, Ch5

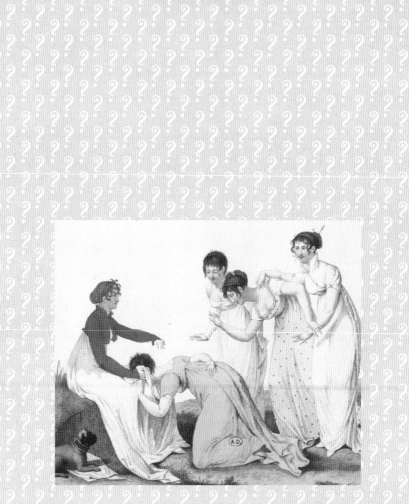

FRIENDS & FAMILY

WITH SEVEN SIBLINGS AND A LIFE SPENT UNDER
THE MAGNIFYING GLASS OF COUNTRY SOCIETY,
JANE AUSTEN WAS WELL QUALIFIED TO ANSWER
ANY DILEMMAS THAT REVOLVE AROUND THE PAIN
AND PLEASURE OF FAMILY AND FRIENDSHIPS.
BRATTISH BROTHER? RECALCITRANT PARENTS?
EMBARRASSING FRIENDS? WEDDING PLANNING
PROBLEMS? EVERYBODY TALKING ABOUT BABIES
BUT YOU? INQUIRE WITHIN.

WHEN SHOULD I TELL MY PARENTS ABOUT MY DEBTS?

THE FACT IS YOU'RE NOT A KID ANYMORE. YOU'VE BEEN OUT ON YOUR OWN, MAKING YOUR OWN WAY WITH WORK AND PLAY FOR QUITE A WHILE NOW, BUT YOU'VE RUN INTO A LITTLE FINANCIAL TROUBLE. YES, MAYBE YOU COULD HAVE MADE A FEW BETTER DECISIONS, POSSIBLY REINED IN THE PLAY A LITTLE BIT, BUT YOU'RE YOUNG AND WANT TO ENJOY LIFE. BE THAT AS IT MAY, YOU'VE GONE AND GOT YOURSELF INTO A FINANCIAL HOLE AND YOU NEED SOME HELP. YOUR PARENTS AREN'T EXACTLY RICH, BUT YOU'RE PRETTY SURE THEY'D GIVE YOU A HAND IF YOU NEEDED IT. WHEN IS THE RIGHT TIME TO BREAK THE BAD NEWS TO THEM?

Few families are untouched by money worries; even Mr. Austen borrowed from relatives. Your answer depends on what your parents are like. If all you have is Lady Bertram, keep quiet—she won't be able to tear herself away from her pug and her couch. If Mrs. Norris is your mom, don't bother—you'll get nothing but a lecture. If you have the same parents as Fanny Price, forget it—you'll have to find your own way out of this. However, if you're very lucky, you'll have Mr. and Mrs. Gardiner, uncle and aunt to the Bennet sisters, as parents, and they will know the best way forward.

A father like Sir Thomas Bertram would bail you out. But you'll have to remember that your salvation might come at a price. When Sir Thomas has to tidy up after his eldest son, it means that younger brother Edmund's future has to be put on hold. Your siblings may resent you for putting a drain on your parents' resources, and with good reason.

Jane Austen's favorite brother Henry got into serious debt. The bank he founded with some friends collapsed. Though Henry had been very ill just before this, and times were hard after the Napoleonic Wars, one can imagine how annoyed people were and how he must have felt. Things had reached a stage, though, where keeping quiet about his troubles was not a possibility; many investors were family and friends.

Jane's will shows us that she didn't forget about the bankruptcy and those who couldn't afford to lose out. She wanted to put things right, so she left money in her will to Madame de Bigeon, Henry's housekeeper as well as to Henry himself, but her affection for her brother was undiminished.

> *"I blush for you, Tom," said he, in his most dignified manner; "I blush for the expedient which I am driven on, and I trust I may pity your feelings as a brother on the occasion. You have robbed Edmund for ten, twenty, thirty years, perhaps for life, of more than half the income which ought to be his ..."*
>
> MANSFIELD PARK

If you are going to tell your parents, the time is now. Perhaps you shouldn't ask them to bail you out, but just let them know what you are going through. If your parents do decide to help you, you must make sure that you pay them back and that they never have to again.

Tom Bertram doesn't learn his lesson when Sir Thomas first picks up his (mighty big) tab. It is only when dissolute living almost kills him that he finally sobers up. Your parents might be wondering whether you'll be the same.

Families should stick together. Your parents will want to know about your troubles and to help if they can, but they won't want a repeat performance. And remember, parents might not always be so sensible —as the years go by, your father may start living like the extravagant Sir Walter Elliot, and another story will unfold.

HOW CAN I MAKE MY FRIEND STOP THE BABY TALK?

YOU UNDERSTAND THAT HAVING A BABY IS A LIFE-CHANGING EVENT, AND YOU'RE PREPARED TO LISTEN TO YOUR PREGNANT FRIEND TALK ABOUT THE EXPERIENCE—A LOT. BUT THE FACT IS YOU'VE NEVER HAD A BABY AND AREN'T REALLY THINKING ABOUT THAT NOW, SO YOU CAN'T RELATE TO HER CONDITION (AND TRUTH BE TOLD, ALL THAT TALK ABOUT NATURAL BIRTHING IS GROSSING YOU OUT). YOU ARE SYMPATHETIC AND INTERESTED, BUT THE CONSTANT BABY BABBLE TO THE EXCLUSION OF EVERYTHING ELSE IS GETTING ON YOUR NERVES. WHAT CAN YOU DO TO CHANGE THE CONVERSATION TO A MORE INCLUSIVE TOPIC?

Jane Austen's letters are peppered with little comments about her sisters-in-law and neighbors who were parents and what they suffered and how tedious the whole business of childbearing was. The fact is, much about childbearing can sound downright disgusting (not to mention traumatizing) to the uninitiated. You shouldn't be surprised that your friend can't think about anything else. And once the baby arrives, don't expect her to talk about anything except the little one.

I suspect that many of the portions of letters that Cassandra destroyed following Jane's death were where Jane was just too bitchy about other people. A few escaped the sisterly scissors: "Mrs Hall of Sherbourn was brought to bed yesterday of a dead child, some weeks before she was expected, oweing to a fright.—I suppose she happened unawares to look at her husband ..." *

* Letter to Cassandra, Steventon, October 27th, 1798

Jane's comments weren't as cruel as she grew older: "Good Mrs. Deedes!—I hope she will get the better of this Marianne [her new baby, her 18th], & then I would recommend to her and Mr. D. the simple regimen of separate rooms." *

In 1817, the year of her death, when she learned of her niece Anna Lefroy's latest pregnancy, she wrote: "Poor Animal, she will be worn out before she is thirty.—I am very sorry for her. Mrs. Clement too is in that way again. I am quite tired of so many children.—Mrs. Benn has a 13th." †

I expect that Jane was feeling dreadful and very weary of anything to do with bodies and doctors. We have to remember that these were private letters. She wouldn't have said anything this rude or cutting to the poor women's faces—she acted as a doting aunt and helpful sister-in-law or friend. You must be like Jane and save your criticisms for yourself or to share only with a person who can be completely trusted to keep quiet about them—and don't ever put them in writing as they may endure for hundreds of years.

* Letter to Fanny Knight, Chawton, February 20th, 1817. † Letter to Fanny Knight, Chawton, March 23rd, 1817

Death from childbirth was a likely fate for any woman in the eighteenth and nineteenth centuries. We know from Jane's pelisse (a gorgeous silk dressing gownish coat in autumnal colors in the Hampshire Museum Service collection) that although she was about 5 feet 7 inches, she had a tiny frame. It's hard to imagine somebody that slender having an easy time if she was ever "brought to bed." Thank goodness she never married, because she would probably have died.

If Jane had voiced some of her thoughts about childbirth and babies, they would have come across as the bitter, cynical opinions of a spinster. She knew enough and was sensitive enough to avoid upsetting any mothers-to-be when there were tragedies, and to share in the joy of new additions to the family. In the box opposite, there is a celebratory poem for her brother, Frank. Her own lovely news about the permanent home she will have at last comes at the end. This Chawton home would see the safe delivery of Jane's "own darling child," *Pride and Prejudice*.

Luckily, Jane had a few trusted confidantes and could use her disgust at the whole icky business of childbearing to populate her novels with some truly horrible children, and some young mothers who are extremely fussy or extremely neglectful and rarely much fun to be with.

Once the children are older, your friend will have other things to talk to you about (very interesting topics, such as schools, lice, and swimming lessons), but for now you must simply smile sweetly, find somebody else to talk to, and perhaps start writing a masterpiece.

My dearest Frank, I wish you joy
Of Mary's safety with a boy,
Whose birth has given little pain,
Compared with that of Mary Jane.
May he a growing Blessing prove,
And well deserve his Parents' Love!
Endow'd with Art's & Nature's Good,
Thy name possessing with thy Blood;
In him, in all his ways, may we
Another Francis William see! —
Thy infant days may he inherit,
Thy warmth, nay insolence of spirit; —
We would not with one fault dispense
To weaken the resemblance.
May he revive thy Nursery sin,
Peeping as daringly within,
(His curley Locks but just descried)
With, "Bet, my be not come to bide."
Fearless of danger, braving pain,
And threatened very oft in vain,
Still may one Terror daunt his soul,
One needful engine of controul
Be found in this sublime array,
A neighbouring Donkey's aweful Bray! —
So may his equal faults as Child
Produce Maturity as mild.

His saucy words & fiery ways
In early Childhood's pettish days
In Manhood shew his Father's mind,
Like him considerate & kind;
All Gentleness to those around,
And eager only not to wound.
Then like his Father too, he must,
To his own former struggles just,
Feel his Deserts with honest Glow,
And all his self-improvement know.
A native fault may thus give birth
To the best blessing, conscious worth. —
As for ourselves, we're very well,
As unaffected prose will tell.
Cassandra's pen will give our state
The many comforts that await
Our Chawton home—how much we find
Already in it, to our mind,
And how convinced that when complete,
It will all other Houses beat
That ever have been made or mended,
With rooms concise, or rooms distended.
You'll find us very snug next year;
Perhaps with Charles & Fanny near
For now it often does delight us
To fancy them just over-right us.

LETTER TO FRANK, CHAWTON, JULY 26TH, 1809

I'VE SAID SOMETHING RUDE.
HOW CAN I MAKE IT BETTER?

YOU'VE DONE IT NOW—YOU'VE PUT YOUR FOOT SQUARELY IN YOUR MOUTH AND OFFENDED SOMEONE. YOU DIDN'T MEAN TO DO IT; IT WASN'T MALICIOUS, BUT YOU WERE TRYING TO IMPRESS A GROUP OF PEOPLE AND, IN SO DOING, YOU JUST SAID SOMETHING A BIT UNFLATTERING ABOUT ONE OF THEIR FRIENDS. NOW THAT PERSON IS CROSS WITH YOU. YOU FEEL TERRIBLE, SO HOW CAN YOU MAKE IT BETTER?

You should feel terrible. And you must expect to be treated terribly, for a little while at least. This is just what happens in *Emma* on the fateful picnic to Box Hill, when the eponymous heroine says a cruel thing (only meaning it as a joke) to poor Miss Bates. It's easy to understand why Emma does it—she's young and inexperienced and she gets carried away by Frank Churchill's flirting and wit: "Frank Churchill grew talkative and gay, making her his first object. Every distinguishing attention that could be paid, was paid to her. To amuse her, and be agreeable in her eyes, seemed all that he cared for ..."*

Being rude to poor Miss Bates is pretty hard to forgive. There is a heavy helping of *l'esprit de l'escalier* in many writers' work, but I suspect that we see the opposite of that here. Perhaps Jane Austen recalled saying something so sharp that it was cruel, and put her feelings of shame and regret to use in the Box Hill incident. When Emma tries to make amends for her bad behavior, she gets a taste of what being the unwanted one must be like, and you are likely to get some of that, too. You'll have to be like Emma and take it on the chin.

E, Ch43

Mr. Knightley steps in after Emma's insensitive blunder. He upbraids her for what she has done, but also tries to reassure Miss Bates that Emma didn't mean the cruel thing she said. Is there somebody you could trust to do the same—tell your victim that you were speaking thoughtlessly and didn't mean it?

> *She was vexed beyond what could have been expressed—almost beyond what she could conceal. Never had she felt so agitated, mortified, grieved, at any circumstance in her life. She was most forcibly struck. The truth of his representation there was no denying. She felt it at her heart. How could she have been so brutal, so cruel to Miss Bates! ... Time did not compose her. As she reflected more, she seemed but to feel it more. She never had been so depressed.*
>
> EMMA

Be careful who you mix with and make jokes in front of in the future and let small acts of kindness and soft words on other subjects soothe the pain you have caused. Some good does come out of Emma's experience—she's nicer to people afterward, and it teaches her how desperately she cares about Mr. Knightley's good opinion of her. Just as Emma later realizes that she shouldn't have trusted Frank Churchill, you shouldn't trust these "acquaintances"— at least one of them is somebody who enjoys playing with people's emotions and stirring up trouble by whispering in others' ears.

Emma immediately starts trying to make amends, but luckily for her there are soon other more important talking points in the busy world of Highbury. Events will move on in your world, too.

CAN I REALLY TEACH AN OLD DOG NEW TRICKS?

Q IT'S COME TO THAT TIME IN LIFE WHEN YOUR PARENTS BECOME THE DEPENDENT ONES AND YOU HAVE TO LOOK AFTER THEM IN MUCH THE WAY THEY LOOKED AFTER YOU ALL THOSE YEARS. AND LIKE CHILDREN, THEY HAVE THEIR OWN ANNOYING HABITS THAT ARE DISRUPTIVE TO YOUR LIFESTYLE—FUSSY EATING, HYPOCHONDRIA, AND FORGETTING TO TURN THE TV OFF, TO MENTION A FEW. YOU WANT TO INTEGRATE THEM INTO YOUR LIFE, NOT LET THEM DICTATE IT. IS THERE A WAY TO GET THEM TO CHANGE THEIR HABITS?

A Mr. Woodhouse's fussiness knows no bounds, but it is Emma's love for her father and the way she cares for him that show us she is not completely spoiled and that she deserves her happy ending. Mr. Woodhouse needs careful management and there is something very sweet in the way that Emma not only puts up with him, but will build her life around him. We can't imagine Frank Churchill agreeing to move in to Hartfield to ensure Mr. Woodhouse's continued happiness, but Mr. Knightley appreciates that Emma will only be happy if her father is happy.

Jane Austen's own mother outlived her. Mrs. Austen was clever and witty, an avid reader and a lover of puzzles and games, but she was clearly difficult, too. Little details included in Jane and Cassandra's letters to each other add up to a lot: "My Mother continues hearty, her appetite & nights are very good, but her Bowels are still not entirely settled, & she sometimes complains of an Asthma, a Dropsy, Water in her Chest & a Liver Disorder." *

* Letter to Cassandra, Steventon, December 18th, 1798

We can sense the way Jane must have been gritting her teeth, but the fact is the sisters did their best for their mother. Jane escaped into her fiction, took long walks, and got up early to play the piano. She fitted her life and work around the demands of her family. Even during her last illness, Jane didn't want to deprive her mother of the couch in the drawing room of their Chawton cottage, and so lay on dining room chairs pushed together.

Time can turn anybody into a fretful Mr. Woodhouse or an annoying Miss Bates. Jane knew others like these. Here she is writing about the impoverished old friend of Martha Lloyd's mother: "Poor Mrs. Stent! It has been her lot to be always in the way; but we must be merciful, for perhaps in time we may come to be Mrs. Stents ourselves, unequal to anything & unwelcome to everybody." *

You can't teach an old dog new tricks; use your imagination and keep in mind that one day the old dog might be you.

Mr. Knightley puts Mr. Woodhouse's and Emma's happiness first:
Mr. Woodhouse taken from Hartfield! No, he felt that it ought not to be attempted. But the plan which had arisen on the sacrifice of this, he trusted his dearest Emma would not find in any respect objectionable; it was, that he should be received at Hartfield; that so long as her father's happiness—in other words his life—required Hartfield to continue her home, it should be his likewise.

EMMA

* Letter to Cassandra, Bath, April 21st, 1805

MY OVERPROTECTIVE FATHER HATES
MY BOYFRIEND—WHAT SHOULD I DO?

Q YOU THINK YOUR BOYFRIEND IS PERFECTION ITSELF. HE'S KIND, ATTENTIVE, ROMANTIC, SWEET—BASICALLY ALL THE GOOD THINGS AND NONE OF THE BAD. SO YOU HAVE A TROUBLE-FREE RELATIONSHIP, RIGHT? WRONG, BECAUSE YOUR FATHER HATES HIM AND MAKES SURE HE KNOWS IT. WHAT CAN YOU POSSIBLY DO TO MAKE YOUR DAD SEE HIM THE WAY THAT YOU DO?

A It's possible that your father is right—perhaps he sees something lacking in your boyfriend that you haven't detected. Maybe you are dating Frank Churchill or Henry Crawford, and your father wants you to hold out for the real thing.

Mr. Woodhouse, for all his fussiness, can see that Frank doesn't quite come up to scratch: "'That young man (speaking lower) is very thoughtless,'" he says. "'Do not tell his father, but that young man is not quite the thing. He has been opening the doors very often this evening, and keeping them open very inconsiderately. He does not think of the draft. I do not mean to set you against him, but indeed he is not quite the thing!'" *

It is going to be almost impossible for Mr. Woodhouse to ever accept Emma marrying—she has been devoted to him for so long and has said that she intends to stay single. Mr. Woodhouse is only persuaded that her marrying is a good thing

* *E*, Ch29

because she chooses Mr. Knightley (whom he has known and trusted for years) and because Mr. Knightley will come and live with them at Hartfield.

The key to getting Mr. Woodhouse's blessing is in ensuring that the status quo is maintained and that his health and security *and* that of those he loves is not adversely affected. He would never be happy to leave Hartfield or for Emma to leave it. The clincher comes when a neighbor's turkeys are stolen, and Mr. Knightley can offer the sense of security that he needs.

Is there something that your beloved does that is turning papa against him? Try to see your boyfriend from your dad's perspective; work out what he

Mrs. Weston's poultry-house was robbed one night of all her turkies—evidently by the ingenuity of man ... Pilfering was housebreaking to Mr. Woodhouse's fears. He was very uneasy; and but for the sense of his son-in-law's protection, would have been under wretched alarm every night of his life ... The result of this distress was, that, with a much more voluntary, cheerful consent than his daughter had ever presumed to hope for at the moment, she was able to fix her wedding-day ...

EMMA

might be doing wrong and how that might be rectified. It might be that your father just needs time to come around to the idea; that would have worked for Emma and Mr. Knightley eventually.

Occasionally we may have to (temporarily anyway) displease our parents—think of Lizzy turning down Mr. Collins: "'An unhappy alternative is before you, Elizabeth.'" Mr. Bennet explains. "'From this day you must be a stranger to one of your parents. Your mother will never see you again if you do *not* marry Mr. Collins, and I will never see you again if you *do*.'" *

* *P&P*, Ch20

CAN A COMPULSIVE BUSYBODY
CHANGE HER WAYS?

YOUR MOM HAS ALWAYS BEEN NOSY, STICKING HER FACE INTO YOUR BUSINESS EVEN WHEN YOU'VE ASKED HER NOT TO. YOU THOUGHT THAT WAS JUST A MOTHER'S PREROGATIVE, BUT YOU'VE RECENTLY BEEN HEARING RUMORS THAT SHE ACTS THIS WAY WITH EVERYONE ELSE, TOO, AND SHE'S GETTING A REPUTATION FOR BEING A GOSSIP AND A NOSY NEIGHBOR. YOU KNOW FIRSTHAND HOW ANNOYING HER BEHAVIOR CAN BE, AND YOU ARE ALSO A LITTLE ASHAMED THAT SHE'S GETTING A BAD NAME. IS THERE A WAY TO GET HER TO TONE IT DOWN?

If you have been hearing rumors about your mother, it means that she's not the only one behaving like this. Almost everybody likes to gossip. Jane Austen said dreadful things when she wrote to Cassandra. She was probably feeling extra mean when she wrote this description of a ball in November 1800: "I believe I drank too much wine last night at Hurstbourne; I know not how else to account for the shaking of my hand to-day … There were very few beauties, and such as there were, were not very handsome. Miss Iremonger did not look well, and Mrs. Blount was the only one much admired. She appeared exactly as she did in September, with the same broad face, diamond bandeau, white shoes, pink husband, and fat neck. The two Miss Coxes

> Mrs. Jennings, Lady Middleton's mother, was a good-humored, merry, fat, elderly woman, who talked a great deal, seemed very happy, and rather vulgar ... She had only two daughters, both of whom she had lived to see respectably married, and she had now therefore nothing to do but marry all the rest of the world. In the promotion of this object, she was zealously active, as far as her ability reached, and missed no opportunity of projecting weddings among all the young people of her acquaintance. She was remarkably quick in the discovery of attachments, and had enjoyed the advantage of raising the blushes and the vanity of many a young lady ...
>
> SENSE AND SENSIBILITY

were there: I traced in one the remains of the vulgar, broad-featured girl who danced at Enham eight years ago; the other is refined into a nice, composed-looking girl, like Catherine Bigg. I looked at Sir Thomas Champneys and thought of poor Rosalie; I looked at his daughter, and thought her a queer animal with a white neck. Mrs. Warren's ... husband is ugly enough, uglier even than his cousin John; but he does not look so *very* old ...The General has got the gout, and Mrs. Maitland the jaundice. Miss Debary, Susan, and Sally, all in black, but without any stature, made their appearance, and I was as civil to them as their bad breath would allow me ..."*

We, of course, shouldn't be reading this. Jane would never have said these things in public, and it's surprising that Cassandra didn't destroy large portions of this letter to safeguard these private thoughts between sisters from future generations of prying eyes. It's interesting that none of Jane's novels are set in Hampshire

* Letter to Cassandra, Steventon, November 20th, 1800

(the county she knew best)—perhaps she didn't want to be accused of poking fun at her neighbors.

Your mother probably won't have realized that she's doing anything wrong. She'll think that she's being kind, helpful, and amusing, just like Mrs. Jennings: "She was full of jokes and laughter, and before dinner was over had said many witty things on the subject of lovers and husbands; hoped they had not left their hearts behind them in Sussex, and pretended to see them blush whether they did or not." *

Each time you see your mother setting off in her merry way, try to very tactfully intervene or change the conversation, in the same way that Lady Middleton (Mrs. Jennings's daughter) does:

"'No bad news, Colonel, I hope,' said Mrs. Jennings, as soon as he entered the room.

'None at all, ma'am, I thank you.'

'Was it from Avignon? I hope it is not to say that your sister is worse.'

'No, ma'am. It came from town, and is merely a letter of business.'

'But how came the hand to discompose you so much, if it was only a letter of business? Come, come, this won't do, Colonel; so let us hear the truth of it.'

'My dear madam,' said Lady Middleton, 'recollect what you are saying.'" †

If your mother can't be persuaded to change her ways, you could try to procure more useful employment for her; this is how an Austen heroine would cope.

* *S&S*, Ch7. †*S&S*, Ch13

Miss Bates "was a great talker upon little matters, which exactly suited Mr. Woodhouse, full of trivial communications and harmless gossip." * Emma (another busybody!) makes clever use of her by constantly entertaining her at Hartfield, an arrangement that suits the older generation well. See if you can use a similar strategy. Where can your mother go to talk as much as she likes and be as nosy as she likes without doing any harm? See if you can find her a Mr. Woodhouse to visit, or even better, a whole establishment of them. Her skills in providing chitchat will be useful, and by choosing to talk to people who rarely go out, her gossiping and mischief-making may go no farther—in fact, she should be valued as an entertaining visitor. Perhaps your mother could become a hospital visitor—a version of the kind but gossipy Nurse Rooke in *Persuasion*, whose information actually proves to be very useful?

> *I had the comfort of finding out the other evening who all the*
> *fat girls with long noses were that disturbed me at the 1st H. ball.*
> *They all prove to be Miss Atkinsons of En—.*
>
> LETTER TO CASSANDRA, STEVENTON, NOVEMBER 21ST, 1800

If she would like to hang out somewhere a little more glamorous, she could become a volunteer in a museum or stately home; her skills in knowing the business of everybody may not be loved by her fellow volunteers, but she could be a real asset as a guide with a detailed knowledge of everybody who has ever lived there, and their affairs and peccadilloes. She can gossip as much as she likes about those who are long dead.

* *E*, Ch3

HOW DO I OUT A CHEATING SPOUSE?

Q YOUR BROTHER'S BEEN MARRIED FOR A NUMBER OF YEARS, AND WHILE YOU'VE NEVER BEEN THE BIGGEST FAN OF HIS WIFE, THINGS SEEMED TO BE GOING WELL— UNTIL RECENTLY. IT'S NOT A SINGLE CLUE YOU CAN PUT YOUR FINGER ON, BUT A NUMBER OF LITTLE THINGS THAT APPEAR TO ADD UP TO ONE BIG THING. YOU SUSPECT SHE'S STRAYED, AND YOU'VE REACHED THE POINT WHERE YOU FEEL THE NEED TO DO SOMETHING ABOUT IT. SHOULD YOU CONFRONT HER OR INFORM YOUR BROTHER OF YOUR SUSPICIONS FIRST?

A People who haven't read Jane Austen's novels often think that they are all about feeble girls wearing bonnets and fainting. Of course, nothing could be farther from the truth. There are dark secrets and adulteries in the plots; it's just that Jane chose not to go into great detail about some things, saying, "Let other pens dwell on guilt and misery. I quit such odious subjects as soon as I can, impatient to restore everybody, not greatly in fault themselves, to tolerable comfort, and to have done with all the rest." * And there is very little fainting.

The consequences of adultery in the eighteenth and nineteenth centuries were dire for women, and the double standard was enshrined in law. A woman could be thrown out, never to see her home and children again, and a man could be sued by the woman's husband or even have to fight a duel.

Readers at the time would have known very well the significance of what Jane suggests with a few deft strokes of the pen. There is the story of Colonel Brandon's ward and Willoughby, of Georgiana Darcy's close call, Lydia Bennet's elopement

* *MP*, Ch48

> *I am proud to say that I have a very good eye at an adulteress, for though*
> *repeatedly assured that another in the same party was the She, I fixed*
> *upon the right one from the first ... she was highly rouged, and looked*
> *rather quietly and contentedly silly than anything else...*
>
> LETTER TO CASSANDRA, BATH, MAY 12TH, 1801

with Wickham, Harriet Smith's anonymous father in *Emma*, William Elliot and Mrs. Clay in *Persuasion*, and then the whole of *Lady Susan* in which the young Jane looked at the career of a very merry widow, the eponymous antiheroine. *Lady Susan* seems a much more eighteenth- than nineteenth-century novel; it's not bawdy exactly, but more so than her later works. Jane was an avid reader of contemporary fiction, and would have kept in step with the change to more moral tastes.

Of course, the results of cheating today are still often grim—heartbreak, unhappiness, miserable children, disruption, separation—and you'd like your brother to avoid all of that.

Jane's characters often have a chance to prevent something happening but don't—where would the story be if they did? The previous misdeeds of a philanderer may be known to somebody, but that person may decide not to say anything, or may say too little too late. In *Persuasion*, Anne Elliot is warned off her cousin William, but her old school friend won't say anything against him until she knows that Anne is not yet engaged.

In *Mansfield Park*, it's possible that Maria Bertram's running away with

Henry Crawford could have been avoided—everybody saw what was going on from the start. Edmund tried, but not terribly hard, to stop his sister from taking part in their dubious amateur theatricals and flirting with Henry. His mother joins in with one of the most feeble appeals to a daughter ever: "'Do not act anything improper, my dear,' said Lady Bertram. 'Sir Thomas would not like it.—Fanny, ring the bell; I must have my dinner.'" *

Henry Crawford knows what he is about. He has planned to make Maria, Julia, and, later, Fanny Price, all a little in love with him. His own sisters know what he is like, but aren't inclined to do very much either. Oh dear. Poor, silly Mr. Rushworth—even he sensed something was wrong—but the marriage between him and Maria was allowed to go ahead. And later, when Maria and Henry are together away from their families, they give in to temptation.

Sir Thomas gets word of what is happening and goes chasing after the adulterers. Note that he doesn't go to Mr. Rushworth—it's Maria he wants to talk to, but sometimes, even if somebody wants to say something, it's too late. Once people are married, intervening between husband and wife is extremely difficult.

Fanny ponders the consequences for everybody: "… it appeared to her that, as far as this world alone was concerned, the greatest blessing to every one of kindred with Mrs. Rushworth would be instant annihilation." †

I think that Jane would advise you to be like Fanny here. Fanny sees that Henry and Mary are no good, and tries to keep some distance—try to do the same with your sister-in-law. Keep in mind that you may be wrong, and don't accuse her of anything. All you have at the moment are suspicions. Fanny was a kind listener to Mr. Rushworth while he was still engaged to Maria, and you can be ready to do that for your brother. Be quiet and watchful, like Fanny, and be ready in case your brother needs your friendship.

MP, Ch15. † *MP*, Ch46

Fanny is there when Edmund needs her as well. We'll assume you aren't secretly in love with your brother, the way Fanny was with her cousin, Edmund, but if you say things against his wife, it may well be interpreted as jealousy. Even though Fanny knows how unprincipled and mercenary Mary is, she holds her tongue—until she feels it is safe to be honest.

> *Fanny, now at liberty to speak openly, felt more than justified in adding to his knowledge of her real character ... Fanny's friendship was all that he had to cling to.*
>
> MANSFIELD PARK

HOW DO I MAKE IT CLEAR THAT
UNMENTIONABLES SHOULD BE UNMENTIONED?

YOUR APARTMENT MATE HAS A HABIT—A LONG-STANDING, DAILY HABIT—OF DRAPING HER WASHED UNDIES AROUND THE APARTMENT TO DRY. IT ISN'T YOUR IDEA OF A TASTEFUL LIVING SPACE, BUT YOU COULD BEAR IT IF IT WEREN'T FOR THE FACT THAT SOMETIMES YOU LIKE TO HAVE FRIENDS OVER. YOUR APARTMENT MATE DOESN'T SEEM TO HAVE A PROBLEM DISPLAYING HER UNMENTIONABLES TO THE WORLD AT LARGE, BUT YOU DO. WHILE YOU'D LIKE TO CONFRONT HER ABOUT IT, YOU DON'T WANT TO SEEM LIKE A WHINING, UPTIGHT PRUDE. WHAT'S THE BEST WAY TO GO ABOUT IT?

Jane Austen would sympathize with you. Her novels are peppered with little scenes of embarrassment. It is family, rather than friends, who tend to be causing the blushes, but that is because the age of the

> *... I called yesterday morning (ought it not in strict propriety to be termed yester-morning?) on Miss Armstrong and was introduced to her father and mother. Like other young ladies she is considerably genteeler than her parents. Mrs. Armstrong sat darning a pair of stockings the whole of my visit. But do not mention this at home, lest a warning should act as an example ...*
>
> LETTER TO CASSANDRA, LYME, SEPTEMBER 14TH, 1804

apartment mate had not yet dawned. Those we live with often seem hell-bent on embarrassing us, and the embarrassment is particularly acute when we are young.

When Jane was staying in Lyme she called on a new friend, a Miss Armstrong. Jane was amused that Miss Armstrong's mother carried on mending stockings, but she wouldn't have wanted her own mother to do the same, and that was clearly a possibility. Mrs. Austen was nobly born. She also had a self-confidence to do things as she pleased. Jane's nephew, James Edward Austen-Leigh, later wrote of Mrs. Austen working in the garden well into her old age, digging potatoes in her green smock, a laborer's garment that she wore to cover her clothes. Jane's mother didn't give a jot what anybody might have thought of her gardening garb.

Fanny Price is faced with domestic disharmony, far worse than the indiscreet mending of underwear, when she goes to stay with her family in Portsmouth: "William was gone: and the home he had left her in was, Fanny could not conceal it from herself, in almost every respect the very reverse of what she could have wished. It was the abode of noise, disorder, and impropriety. Nobody was in their right place, nothing was done as it ought to be. She could not respect her parents as she had hoped." *

Fanny hates it there, and her parents aren't interested in getting to know her better: "She might scruple to make use of the words, but she must and did feel that her mother was a partial, ill-judging parent, a dawdle, a slattern, who neither taught nor restrained her children, whose house was the scene of mismanagement and discomfort from beginning to end ..." †

So what does Fanny do? These are terrible feelings to have about your own mother, and her father was worse, and certainly not going to be the source of any

* *MP*, Ch39. † Ibid.

improvement to things. Fanny doesn't want to seem like a snob, and she certainly isn't going to voice her critical opinions. She doesn't quietly seethe, or collapse into despair, or join in the arguments; she responds in a practical way: "Fanny was very anxious to be useful, and not to appear above her home, or in any way disqualified or disinclined, by her foreign education, from contributing her help to its comforts, and therefore set about working …" *

You aren't Fanny reunited with a mother you haven't seen for years. This is your apartment mate and it's your home, too. You can (very tactfully) say something, but better still do something positive to bring about a change. First of all, Fanny throws herself into the work of the house, sewing and helping to get things ready for her brother, Sam, who is off to sea. Then she does what she can to restore harmony between her two younger sisters. She sees where she can make the most difference, and that's with Susan. She sets about making the room they are sharing much more congenial. She joins the library and helps Susan to become a reader and discover that there is much more to life than frustration and mending: "By sitting together upstairs, they avoided a great deal of the disturbance of the house; Fanny had peace, and Susan learned to think it no misfortune to be quietly employed … By degrees the girls came to spend the chief of the morning upstairs, at first only in working and talking …" †

Fanny is tactful, but she's active in dealing with the problems. This is a big turnaround for her—previously she's been somebody who watched, did other people's bidding, or very quietly resisted things. Fanny finds that she can take action to change things, and she loves it. She creates areas of harmony in the chaotic house and then she joins the library and is "amazed at being anything *in propria persona*, amazed at her own doings in every way, to be a renter, a chuser of books!" ‡ Seemingly small actions can make a huge difference.

* *MP*, Ch39, † *MP*, Ch40. ‡ Ibid.

Fanny's time in Portsmouth helps her become more the mistress of her own destiny—a person in her own right. She doesn't have to put up with the status quo, and nor do you. Be as gentle and practical as Fanny, but take some action. A clothes horse or dryer of some kind won't be terribly expensive, and soon you won't be mortified if one of the Crawfords shows up uninvited. Creating harmony is all in being efficient and practical; Jane went from writing, to mending, to reading the latest best seller all in one morning. You can achieve this balance, too.

Do not be angry with me for beginning another letter to you. I have read the "Corsair," mended my petticoat, and have nothing else to do.

LETTER TO CASSANDRA, LONDON, MARCH 5TH, 1814

HOW DO I SWAP A "FRIEND" DATE FOR A ROMANTIC DATE?

Q YOU DIDN'T HAVE A DATE FOR YOUR SCHOOL REUNION AND NEITHER DID YOUR BEST MALE FRIEND, SO YOU AGREED TO GO TOGETHER. THERE'S NO ROMANTIC UNDERCURRENT TO THIS—YOU'VE BEEN CLOSE FRIENDS SINCE ELEMENTARY SCHOOL—SO THAT ISN'T AN ISSUE. THE PROBLEM IS THAT AFTER YOU AGREED TO GO WITH YOUR FRIEND, A MAN YOU'VE HAD A CRUSH ON FOR AGES SAID HE'D GO WITH YOU. YOU'D LOVE TO ROCK UP SHOWING OFF YOUR NEW BEAU, BUT CAN YOU REALLY DITCH YOUR FRIEND WITHOUT HURTING HIS FEELINGS?

A Tread carefully; you may find that your friend has just been too shy to make his true feelings known. Edmund Bertram and Fanny Price were somewhat like you two. They were brought up together and nobody expected them to fall in love. In fact, one of the reasons for Fanny coming to live at Mansfield Park was to save her rich cousins from marrying her later!

Horrible Aunt Norris was wrong about this, and just about everything else too: "'The very idea of her having been suffered to grow up at a distance from us all in poverty and neglect, would be enough to make either of the dear, sweet-tempered boys in love with her,'" she advises Sir Thomas. "'But breed her up with them from this time, and suppose her even to have the beauty of an angel, and she will never be more to either than a sister.'" *

You have said that you will go to this event with your best friend, and go with him you must. How would you feel if he dumped you and you had nobody to

* MP, Ch1*

go with? The only possible way you can go with this new romantic prospect (who may well turn out to be a John Thorpe, Henry Crawford, Willoughby, or Wickham) is if your friend has someone else who he actually wants to go with, too. You could possibly go as a foursome or in a group, but remember that your commitment to your friend should come first.

Fanny wisely keeps quiet about her love for Edmund until it is reciprocated. He treats her so thoughtlessly once Mary Crawford arrives on the scene, that it's a wonder she carries on loving him. He is a bit of a dolt, but there are other friends, far falser, in Jane Austen's work. Perhaps Isabella Thorpe, "friend" of Catherine Morland, is the worst of

Edmund Bertram abandons Fanny Price on their day out to be with Mary Crawford: *Fanny's thoughts were now all engrossed by the two who had left her so long ago, and getting quite impatient, she resolved to go in search of them. She followed their steps along the bottom walk, and had just turned up into another, when the voice and the laugh of Miss Crawford once more caught her ear ... the result of the whole was to her disappointment and depression ...*

MANSFIELD PARK

them all. She plots and uses Catherine and tries to persuade her to break her prior engagements to do things with her instead.

The gender of your friend is irrelevant. Jane would consider that what matters is that you behave as a true friend should. Your possible date may not understand, but he'll just have to wait for another occasion. You must be as steadfast as Catherine and explain the situation: "'Do not urge me, Isabella,' she says. 'I am engaged to Miss Tilney. I cannot go.'" *

* NA, Ch13

TO TATTOO OR NOT TO TATTOO?

Q YOU ARE DESPERATE TO GET A TATTOO. YOU'VE SAVED UP ENOUGH MONEY AND YOU KNOW EXACTLY WHAT YOU WANT—IT'S SOMETHING TASTEFUL, MEANINGFUL, AND COMMEMORATIVE, SO YOU KNOW YOU'D BE HAPPY TO HAVE IT FOR THE REST OF YOUR LIFE. HOWEVER, YOUR PARENTS DON'T CARE HOW RESPONSIBLE AND THOUGHTFUL YOU'VE BEEN ABOUT THIS (PERMANENT) DECISION. THEY ARE COMPLETELY AGAINST THE IDEA. HOW DO YOU CONVINCE THEM THAT YOU'RE MAKING THE RIGHT DECISION?

A You will not convince them, so you will just have to decide what you would like to do. If you are old enough to legally get a tattoo, you are also old enough to make your own mind up about it; however, you are right not to want to upset your parents—a heroine shouldn't. Even where the parents are ineffectual (the Bennets, Lady Bertram), demanding (Mr. Woodhouse), or positively unpleasant (Mr. Price), their daughters still try to treat them with consideration and respect.

Jane Austen was a clergyman's daughter, and she had been brought up to honor her father and mother, but it wasn't all about being a goody-goody. We know that she didn't always find life with her mother easy.

If you really want to go against your parents' wishes, you can quietly go ahead; but you need not flaunt the result or ever have it on show for them. Be discreet.

Your parents might be particularly overprotective like Mr. Woodhouse, who was deeply distressed at the thought of Emma, who is planning a dance, catching cold if anything as reckless as dancing in a passageway occurred: "'Oh! no,' said he; 'it would be the extreme of imprudence. I could not bear it for Emma! Emma is not strong. She would catch a dreadful cold. So would poor little Harriet. So you would all … do not let them talk of such a wild thing.'" *

Emma manages it in the end by working around her father's concerns. She cleverly offsets his worry about the location with his concern about the horses: "'… papa, it will be very

> Sensible Elinor Dashwood knows that the wishes of parents and children are unlikely to coincide:
> *"The old well established grievance of duty against will, parent against child, was the cause of all."*
> SENSE AND SENSIBILITY

convenient for the horses. They will be so near their own stable.'" † But the clincher is that Mrs. Weston will be in charge. Emma knows that her father will think it is okay if Mrs. Weston ("who is carefulness itself" ‡) is in control.

Imagine how Mr. Woodhouse would feel if Emma decided to get a tattoo! It would have to be done with the utmost discretion or Mr. Woodhouse would become distressed. That said, if Emma were able to tell her father that Mrs. Weston had a tattoo and would go with her to the tattoo salon, she would probably get her way.

As Jane grew older, she understood very well how mistakes could be made while young. Having observed her beloved niece, Fanny, going shopping, Jane wrote: "I consider it as a thing of course at her time of life—one of the sweet taxes of youth to choose in a hurry and make bad bargains."§

Don't make your mind up in a hurry—at least an ill-chosen cloth cap and a gown are not permanent.

* *E*, Ch29 † Ibid. ‡ Ibid. § Letter to Cassandra, Godmersham Park, September 23rd, 1813

WHAT TO DO ABOUT A SPONGING BROTHER?

 SOMETIMES YOU WONDER IF MEN ARE JUST NATURALLY LAZIER THAN WOMEN. THAT MIGHT BE AN UNFAIR GENERALIZATION, BUT IT CERTAINLY APPLIES TO YOUR BROTHER, WHO TAKES EVERY OPPORTUNITY TO BORROW MONEY, CRASH AT YOUR PLACE FOR WEEKS AND STEAL FOOD OUT OF YOUR REFRIGERATOR. YOU ARE REALLY NOT PLEASED WITH HIS BEHAVIOR, BUT HE IS FAMILY, AFTER ALL. WHAT'S THE BEST WAY TO PUT A STOP TO YOUR BROTHER'S SPONGING WITHOUT ALIENATING HIM?

 I wonder if your brother is a Tom Bertram or only a Henry Austen. If he's a Tom Bertram, you are in for trouble. The plot of *Mansfield Park* takes off because of Tom's bad behavior and his father having to pay off his debts. Tom gets a dressing down—he has "robbed Edmund for ten, twenty, thirty years, perhaps for life, of more than half the income which ought to be his." *

Sir Thomas thinks his son should be mortified and change his ways, but it will take more than this for Tom to start acting responsibly. It is only after a whole novel,

* *MP*, Ch3

a brush with death, and seeing what becomes of his similarly unprincipled sister that Tom starts behaving as he should. He has to hit rock bottom in order to see sense. Another trip to the races, an accident, and "a good deal of drinking" mean that he almost dies. When he's abandoned by his friends, it is Edmund who goes to look after him and bring him home. Edmund does this because Tom is his brother and he wants to save his mother from distress—but tough love is required.

I don't think Jane Austen would advise you to cut your brother off completely—families in her novels stick together, but action to protect the interests of innocent parties is taken. If your brother is as bad as Tom Bertram, Jane would encourage you to try to make sure that he doesn't bring the family down with him.

> *"Tom listened with some shame and some sorrow; but escaping as quickly as possible, could soon with cheerful selfishness reflect, firstly, that he had not been half so much in debt as some of his friends; secondly, that his father had made a most tiresome piece of work of it ..."*
>
> MANSFIELD PARK

Let's hope that your brother is more of a Henry Austen. He wasn't a sponger, but he certainly caused plenty of worry and sometimes cost the family a lot. Henry was the most fun of the Austen brothers, and Jane stayed with him in London while she was working with her publishers. It was Henry who oversaw the publication of *Persuasion* and *Northanger Abbey* after her death, Henry who couldn't resist leaking the secret of who the best-selling author was, Henry who tried his hand at many professions, and Henry who went bankrupt. But even when that happened, the Austens still forgave him. He was their Henry—and "Oh, what a Henry!" * as Jane wrote to Cassandra when she heard of him dancing at the most glamorous of parties.

* Letter to Cassandra, Chawton, June 23rd, 1814

I think Jane would say that you should try to put up with your brother's faults because he is your brother; but that a bad brother shouldn't be allowed to push his sister around. An Austen heroine would stand up to a manipulator, the way that Elizabeth Bennet stands up to Lady Catherine de Bourgh. A time comes when you have to draw the line.

Wickham is the worst (quasi-) brother in Jane's work. He has been brought up with many of the privileges of a son at Pemberley, but he tries to seduce Georgiana. When this happens, Mr. Darcy wants to have nothing more to do with him, and Wickham is banished from Pemberley. Mr. Darcy will still act in a principled way, however, for the good of those he loves. Mrs. Lydia Wickham is allowed to come to Pemberley by herself, and Elizabeth sometimes helps them out financially, but Wickham has blown it forever. Decide where your line is, and don't let your brother cross it.

You may have to employ the principle of less eligibility. The word "eligible" often occurs in Jane's work. The "most eligible" thing was the one worth choosing. This principle of less eligibility was drawn from the work of the philosopher Jeremy Bentham, who was a contemporary of Jane's, to become enshrined in laws governing the treatment of criminals and the poor. The idea was that workhouses and prisons should be deterrents—people wouldn't allow themselves to end up in a place where life was more unpleasant than if they were doing the worst possible job. And there were some pretty horrible jobs.

Try embracing this philosophy and put it into practice when your brother descends on you. Make sure that there is nowhere comfortable to sleep and that you don't keep restocking the refrigerator with things that he likes. Replacing the beer with wheatgrass juice should work. He will probably find that less eligible and soon be on his way. However, remember that he is your brother; with some more careful management, he may become just as much fun as Henry Austen.

With so many brothers, Jane would have understood just how you felt. Brothers can be spoiled and selfish or the best friends of one's life. At least yours isn't likely to turn into James Austen. Here is Jane anticipating another visit from him: "I am sorry and angry that his Visits should not give one more pleasure; the company of so good and clever a Man ought to be gratifying in itself; –but his Chat seems all forced, his Opinions on many points too much copied from his Wife's, and his time here is spent I think in walking about the House & banging the Doors, or ringing the Bell for a glass of water." *

* Letter to Cassandra, Southampton, February 8th, 1807

77

HOW CAN I DELETE A CONTACT ON FACEBOOK WITHOUT CAUSING OFFENSE?

IN THESE DAYS OF SOCIAL NETWORKING, CAN YOU DECIDE NOT TO BE FRIENDS WITH PEOPLE WITHOUT UPSETTING THEM? ONE FRIEND IN PARTICULAR IS GETTING ON YOUR NERVES. IT'S NOT THAT YOU DISLIKE THIS FRIEND EXACTLY; IT'S JUST THAT YOU'VE GROWN TIRED OF HER CONSTANT UPDATES BEMOANING THE WORLD AND SHARED LINKS TO NONSENSE WEBSITES. IS IT POSSIBLE TO "UNFRIEND" HER ON FACEBOOK WITHOUT HURTING HER FEELINGS?

> *Mr Elton ... not only sat at her elbow, but was continually obtruding his happy countenance on her notice, and solicitously addressing her upon every occasion ... and made it some effort with her to preserve her good manners. For her own sake she could not be rude ... Mr. Elton's civilities were dreadfully ill-timed; but she had the comfort of appearing very polite, while feeling very cross.*
>
> EMMA

The continual obtruding of your friend's countenance may be annoying, but you must, like Emma, make sure that you preserve your good manners and the comfort of appearing polite, while finding a way out of the situation. Although some of the mechanics of managing friendships have changed, the principles of politeness and its importance have not.

When Jane Austen was advising her niece, Anna, on a novel in progress, she was eager to point out some of the etiquette mistakes she had made: "I have also scratched out the introduction between Lord Portman and his brother and Mr. Griffin. A country surgeon ... would not be introduced to men of their rank, and when Mr. P. is first brought in, he would not be introduced as the Honourable." and "We think you had better not leave England. Let the Portmans go to Ireland; but as you know nothing of the manners there, you had better not go with them. You will be in danger of giving false representations. Stick to Bath and the Foresters. There you will be quite at home." *

What Jane was saying is that seemingly small matters of politeness can have a huge impact in life and in writing convincing fiction. She was also telling Anna how important it is to stick to the rules of society, because they are there to avoid people getting hurt or offended.

The astonishingly rude Lady Catherine de Bourgh would delete or "unfriend" somebody without a second thought—she wouldn't care about the hurt it might cause or the repercussions, but it does her no good in the long run.

Her rudeness, in this case to Elizabeth Bennet, knows no bounds: "'I take no leave of you, Miss Bennet; I send no compliments to your mother ...'" †

Elizabeth is smarter and proves to be better at navigating society's choppy waters. She knows that it's best to be polite while subtly maintaining one's privacy settings. Lydia is desperate to share some news when they meet for lunch at a coaching inn, but Jane and Elizabeth first tell the waiter he need not stay at the table—they're trying to stop their younger sisters from gossiping in public.

Jane wouldn't advise you to make a big rude gesture to get this person's tedious musings out of your life—she would tell you to stick to the basic rules of good manners, and then to quietly and discreetly block the incessant updates.

* Letters to Anna Austen, Chawton, August 17th & 18th, 1814. † *P&P*, Ch56

HOW DO I KEEP MY DAD FROM EMBARRASSING ME?

YOU LOVE YOUR FATHER TO PIECES JUST AS HE IS, BUT AS MUCH AS YOU HATE TO ADMIT IT, THERE IS THAT ONE LITTLE THING YOU'D LIKE TO ALTER SLIGHTLY: HIS DRESS SENSE. HE'S NOT EVEN THAT OLD, AND YET HE DRESSES LIKE AN OCTOGENARIAN WHO'S GIVEN UP ON LIFE. WHAT CAN YOU DO TO MAKE HIM WISEN UP TO HIS APPEARANCE SO YOU DON'T FEEL EMBARRASSED BEING SEEN WITH HIM IN PUBLIC?

Think about the fathers in Jane Austen's novels, and you'll find that you have got off lightly. We have Mr. Bennet, who hides in his library; Mr. Woodhouse, who is gentle, but very high maintenance; Harriet Smith's invisible father; General Tilney, who is motivated only by money; Mr. Price, who either ignores Fanny or makes crude remarks; Sir Thomas Bertram, who takes a whole novel to wake up; and Elinor and Marianne Dashwood's father, who is dead. In terms of being good parents, they are almost all useless or absent.

Sir Walter Elliot in *Persuasion* is perhaps the worst. He has lived in such an extravagant way that the family home has to be rented out. He favors his first born, the similarly vain Elizabeth, and has little time for his married daughter, Mary (whose looks have, he thinks, grown coarse), but the one who receives the worst treatment is his middle daughter, who "with an elegance of mind and sweetness of character, which must have placed her high with any people of real understanding, was nobody with either father or sister; her word had no weight; her convenience was always to give way—she was only Anne." *

When Admiral and Mrs. Croft become the tenants of the Elliots' home, Kellynch Hall, Jane shows just how a man like Sir Walter appears to outsiders. The friendly Crofts are telling Anne about the little changes they have made:"'. . . I have done very little besides sending away some of the large looking glasses from my dressing room, which was your father's. A very good man, and very much the gentleman I am sure; but I should think, Miss Elliot,' (looking with serious reflection), 'I should think he must be rather a dressy man for his time of life. Such a number of looking-glasses! oh Lord! there was no getting away from oneself. So I got Sophy to lend me a hand, and we soon shifted their quarters; and now I am quite snug, with my little shaving glass in one corner . . .'

Anne, amused in spite of herself, was rather distressed for an answer . . ."†

* *P*, Ch1. † *P*, Ch13

> *Vanity was the beginning and the end of Sir Walter Elliot's character; vanity of person and of situation. He had been remarkably handsome in his youth; and, at fifty-four, was still a very fine man. Few women could think more of their personal appearance than he did . . .*
>
> PERSUASION

Anne could be dying of embarrassment here, but she knows that she can't control her father's vanity or looks, and that good people like the Crofts won't be judging her by them. Your situation might seem the opposite of Anne's, but which father would you rather have, your own or Sir Walter?

Jane doesn't go into much detail about the clothes and appearances of other heroines' fathers because it just isn't important. Many things are more important than wearing fashionable clothes. Marianne Dashwood grows to love Colonel Brandon although he likes "flannel waistcoats" (vests), and nobody is asking you to fall in love with your dad!

Your father is probably more like Mr. Woodhouse than any of the others. He's getting on a little and he worries constantly about people being too cold, but Emma wouldn't give him a makeover. We can imagine her taking him to Macy's to buy new versions of the clothes he loves, or else she would choose presents for him— perhaps the softest, warmest scarf, corduroy pants just the same as the ones he's always liked, a cashmere cardigan—but she wouldn't hassle him or try to change him. She'd know, just as Anne Elliot does, that people whose love and friendship are worth keeping aren't going to judge her by her father's appearance.

Jane Austen's parents' marriage was a happy one. Her own father was already in his mid-forties when she was born, already older than she would ever be.

As well as being a clergyman, he took in pupils, and so Jane grew up in a busy family home that was also a small boarding school. She was probably like Catherine Morland, who loved cricket, baseball, and "rolling down the green slope at the back of the house." Jane's father encouraged her reading and her writing, and seems to have been nothing like the selfish parents in her novels. He tried to interest a publisher in *First Impressions*. He was clever and kind. And just by the way, he was also good looking. When he was young and at Oxford, he was known as "the Handsome Proctor." It's no wonder that witty, nobly born Cassandra Leigh fell in love with him.

Jane's niece, Anna, recalled his lovely white hair and hazel eyes. There's no mention of his clothes.

As a young man I have always understood that he was considered extremely handsome, and it was a beauty which stood by him all his life. At the time when I have the most perfect recollection of him he must have been hard upon seventy, but his hair in its milk-whiteness might have belonged to a much older man. It was very beautiful, with short curls about the ears. His eyes were not large, but of a peculiar and bright hazel. My aunt Jane's were something like them, but none of the children had precisely the same excepting my uncle Henry.

RECOLLECTION OF ANNA LEFROY, NÉE AUSTEN, IN HILL, C. (1923)

You need to focus on what is important here, and that is that your father is a lovely man and a good dad. Buy him some presents if you want to, but don't try to change him.

IS IT TIME TO MOVE IN
WITH MY BOYFRIEND AND KIDS?

YOU AND YOUR BOYFRIEND ARE BOTH DIVORCEES WITH CHILDREN FROM PREVIOUS MARRIAGES. YOU'RE READY TO TAKE THE NEXT STEP AND MOVE IN TOGETHER, BUT YOU'RE WORRIED ABOUT THE CHILDREN AND IF THEY'LL GET ALONG. THE KIDS ARE ABOUT THE SAME AGE BUT GO TO DIFFERENT SCHOOLS AND MIX IN DIFFERENT SOCIAL CIRCLES, AND THEY AREN'T TOO HOT ON THE IDEA OF LIVING TOGETHER. SHOULD YOU GO AHEAD ANYWAY AND HOPE THAT IN TIME THEY'LL LEARN TO GET ALONG?

Divorce was rare in Jane Austen's time, but second marriages were common. With so many women dying in childbirth, and mortality rates generally much higher than today, men often married again and many children had stepmothers. Of course, there were many widows looking for second husbands, too, so mixed-up families were very common.

Jane's brother, James, lost his first wife and was left with a small daughter, Anna. He tried to woo his cousin, Eliza, but she turned him down. Instead, he married Mary Lloyd, sister of Martha (Jane's best friend), and had two further children.

Jane didn't like Mary and clearly felt sorry for Anna, who often sought sanctuary with her aunts. I suspect there are echoes of Mary moving into the rectory at Steventon in the opening of *Sense and Sensibility*, where Fanny Dashwood arrives and takes possession of it with insensitive haste.

Elinor and Marianne Dashwood feel like visitors in their own home, and are then pushed out of it. John Dashwood, the person now in control of the family fortune, does almost nothing to make sure that they will be secure or happy. His horrible wife talks him out of giving them proper financial security, and he ends up doing little more than "helping them to move their things, and sending them presents of fish and game, and so forth, whenever they are in season ..."*

Remember that your children are not choosing this new situation, and may feel, just as Elinor, Marianne, Margaret, and their mother do, that they are being steamrollered into something. John and

Mrs. John Dashwood now installed herself mistress of Norland; and her mother [-in-law] and sisters-in-law were degraded to the condition of visitors ... It was very well known that no affection was ever supposed to exist between the children of any man by different marriages ...

SENSE AND SENSIBILITY

Fanny Dashwood have a legal right to Norland, the gorgeous family home, but they don't actually *need* it, and they certainly don't need to be so speedy about moving in.

Fanny Dashwood is horrible and so is her mother, Mrs. Ferrars. The reader longs for them to get their comeuppance: "Elinor's curiosity to see Mrs. Ferrars was satisfied. She had found in her everything that could tend to make a farther connection between the families undesirable. She had seen enough of her pride, her meanness, and her determined prejudice against herself, to comprehend all the difficulties that must have perplexed the engagement, and retarded the marriage of Edward and herself, had he been otherwise free ..."†

Jane's novels often concern children whose parents have acted hastily, incautiously, or wrongly. If you try to do things too quickly, you'll seem as mean and selfish as Fanny Dashwood and her horrible mother. Jane would advise you to proceed with extreme caution.

* *S&S*, Ch2. † *S&S*, Ch35

MY FRIEND KEEPS TURNING UP AND WON'T LEAVE. WHAT SHOULD I DO?

YOU LOVE SPENDING TIME WITH YOUR FRIENDS, ALL OF THEM, BUT THERE'S ONE FRIEND WHO INVITES HERSELF OVER AND DOESN'T SEEM TO RECOGNIZE WHEN THE PARTY'S OVER. IN FACT, SHE HAS A TENDENCY TO OUTSTAY HER WELCOME BY HOURS. YOU DON'T MIND HER COMING OVER, BUT ONLY WHEN SHE'S EXPECTED, AND YOU JUST WISH YOU COULD GET HER TO LEAVE WHEN IT'S TIME INSTEAD OF WELL PAST. HOW DO YOU KEEP HER VISITS UNDER CONTROL AND GIVE HER THE BOOT WITHOUT MAKING HER FEEL UNWELCOME?

Matters like this were much easier to manage in Jane Austen's time. Today, the informality of most social interaction means that situations like yours are harder to handle, but there have always been people who outstay their welcome, and don't realize or don't care that they are crossing the boundaries of polite behavior. Etiquette is meant to make life pleasanter for everybody—it isn't meant to be about snobbery and one-upmanship.

Mrs. Bennet usually tried to keep to the rules, but at the Netherfield Ball she oversteps the mark, thinking that her daughters will be seen to advantage if they leave later than everybody else. Elizabeth reads the situation properly and is mortified. You are much more like Mr. Bingley than his horrible sisters in wanting to avoid returning rudeness with hostility, but you may have to keep this strategy in reserve if all others fail. When Mr. Bingley and Jane Bennet are married, they are so polite that they won't even ask Lydia and Wickham to leave! The Wickhams "frequently staid so long, that even Bingley's good humor was overcome, and he proceeded so far as to *talk* of giving them a hint to be gone." *

> *The Longbourn party were the last of all the company to depart, and by a maneuver of Mrs. Bennet, had to wait for their carriages a quarter of an hour after everybody else was gone, which gave them time to see how heartily they were wished away by some of the family. Mrs. Hurst and her sister scarcely opened their mouths, except to complain of fatigue, and were evidently impatient to have the house to themselves.*
>
> PRIDE AND PREJUDICE

Perhaps you could have a word with a friend who *does* abide by the rules and ask her to help you make the boundaries clearer. Even if friends arrive separately, they could leave together. Perhaps somebody could (very firmly) offer to give your lurking friend a lift home. (Think of how in *Emma* the people of Highbury look after each other, working together to take care of Miss Bates.)

Even a person as nasty as Fanny Dashwood understands how people are meant to behave. When she calls on Elinor and Marianne in London, she obeys the rules, although she's lousy company. Fifteen minutes was the minimum amount of time

* *P&P*, Ch61

it was acceptable to stay: "Mrs. John Dashwood ... appeared nothing more than a little proud-looking woman of uncordial address, who met her husband's sisters without any affection, and almost without having anything to say to them; for of the quarter of an hour bestowed on Berkeley Street, she sat at least seven minutes and a half in silence." *

Jane's contemporary readers would have understood the code and what was expected of everybody. The rules were more relaxed for relatives and old friends; people might stay weeks, but this was meant to be by mutual agreement. Some people would always show up when they weren't really wanted. I don't think Jane was always thrilled to see her brother, James. "James seems to have taken to his old trick of coming to Steventon in spite of Mary's [his second wife's] reproaches, for he was here before breakfast and is now paying us a second visit." †

It was easier in Jane's time to say that you weren't in if you didn't want to see somebody. Ladies would have days when they were "at home" to receive callers. If a person whom one didn't wish to see came calling, they could be turned away by a servant who would take the unwanted visitor's card. When Catherine Morland is desperate to see her friend Eleanor to explain why she stood her up, she rushes past the servant in a way that would be considered rude, but her desperation to make amends and explain herself can be excused. She says: "I am come in a great hurry—It was all a mistake ... —I would not stay for the servant." ‡

You may not have a servant to say that you aren't home, but you can make creative use of technology instead. You could update your Facebook status to show the world when you're busy. You could perhaps set an "out-of-office auto reply" on your e-mails, or get your phone to ring you when you need an excuse.

You should also remember that not all social engagements have to take place at home. You could arrange to meet your friend at the theater, at a public place

* S&S, Ch34. † Letter to Cassandra, Steventon, October 27th, 1798. ‡ NA, Ch13

(the equivalent of the Assembly Rooms in Bath), or on a picnic, perhaps to Box Hill. Make sure that you arrive in separate carriages and that you will leave that way, too, so that she has no opportunity to impose on you.

I'm afraid that if all of these methods fail, you may end up having to act as rudely as General Tilney when he wants to get rid of Catherine Morland. His daughter Eleanor is given the unpleasant task of telling her friend that the visit is being brought to an abrupt end. If all else fails, call her a taxi.

> Eleanor Tilney has to tell Catherine the bad news:
> *"But—how can I tell you?—tomorrow morning is fixed for your leaving us, and not even the hour is left to your choice; the very carriage is ordered, and will be here at seven o'clock, and no servant will be offered you."*
>
> NORTHANGER ABBEY

HOW CAN I GET MY FRIEND TO
STOP BEING OBSESSED WITH BOYS?

 HIGH SCHOOL WAS A WHILE AGO AND YOUR PRIORITIES HAVE CHANGED. YOU'RE INTO ART, FILM, LITERATURE, THEATER, PROGRESSING IN YOUR CAREER—ALL THE THINGS THAT MAKE LIFE RICH AND VARIED. YOU AND MOST OF YOUR FRIENDS LOVE TO TALK ABOUT EVERYTHING AND ANYTHING UNDER THE SUN, BUT THERE'S ONE FRIEND OF YOURS WHO SEEMS TO BE STUCK AT HER HIGH SCHOOL PROM. SHE TALKS SOLELY OF GETTING BOYFRIENDS, HAVING BOYFRIENDS, AND LOSING BOYFRIENDS, AND HER INANE BABBLING IS DRIVING EVERYONE CRAZY. CAN YOU GET HER TO EXPLORE OTHER TOPICS OF CONVERSATION OR DO YOU HAVE TO START "FORGETTING" TO INVITE HER TO LUNCH?

Jane Austen loved dancing and flirting, and even as she aged, she never lost her respect for these pursuits. Here she is talking about a girl called Harriot Bridges, whose three elder sisters had married very young: "She goes on now as young ladies of seventeen ought to do, admired and admiring." *

By then, Jane was twenty-three and teenage obsessions were behind her. She was well on the way to finishing her third novel. Your friend sounds like the appalling Anne Steele in *Sense and Sensibility*. Such behavior should be grown out of.

The moment Anne opens her mouth, we see just how stupid and shallow she is. The poor thing is still unattached at the end of the novel, and still chasing

---

* Letter to Cassandra, Steventon, Christmas Eve 1798

Anne Steele can talk of nothing but beaux:

"I'm sure there's a vast many smart beaux in Exeter; but you know, how could I tell what smart beaux there might be about Norland? and I was only afraid the Miss Dashwoods might find it dull at Barton, if they had not so many as they used to have. But perhaps you young ladies may not care about the beaux, and had as lief be without them as with them. For my part, I think they are vastly agreeable, provided they dress smart and behave civil. But I can't bear to see them dirty and nasty."

SENSE AND SENSIBILITY

after a beau. Your friend will probably be the same unless she calms down and finds some other interests. Try to help her to do this before you resort to the more desperate measure of dumping her entirely. If you are clever, you may be able to employ a strategy that will either improve her or drive her away. Try starting a book club and for your first choice—*Sense and Sensibility*.

She may not recognize her character type in fiction, but if she hates reading, she can choose not to come and hurrah!—you are free of her for at least one evening each month. If she does come and starts going on and on about boyfriends, do what Anne's sister, Lucy, does—try to change the subject: "'Lord! Anne,' cried her sister, 'you can talk of nothing but beaux; —you will make Miss Dashwood believe you think of nothing else.' And then to turn the discourse, she began admiring the house and the furniture." *

Eventually, your friend should get the message, or else find your company so dull that she'll seek other friends who share her obsession.

* *S&S*, Ch21

IS INVITING KIDS TO MY WEDDING
A LOVELY IDEA OR A BIG MISTAKE?

YOU'RE DUE TO GET MARRIED VERY SHORTLY AND, LIKE EVERYTHING ELSE SURROUNDING THE WEDDING, THERE'S DRAMA ABOUT THE GUEST LIST. YOU AND YOUR PARTNER WANT A LOW-STRESS CEREMONY AND A GREAT PARTY AFTER, BUT YOUR FAMILY IS DETERMINED TO INCLUDE THE YOUNGER GENERATION IN THE FESTIVITIES. YOU HAVE NOTHING AGAINST KIDS, BUT YOU'VE WITNESSED FIRSTHAND THE CARNAGE THAT A GAGGLE OF LITTLE ONES RIDING SUGAR HIGHS CAN INFLICT ON A WEDDING. NATURALLY, YOU'RE WORRIED THEY MIGHT RUIN YOUR SPECIAL DAY. IF YOU GIVE IN, WILL YOU REGRET INVITING CHILDREN FOR THE REST OF YOUR MARRIED LIFE?

In a few years' time, you could be on the other end of this. You might be invited to a wedding and realize that although you'd like to attend, you can't because the bride and groom are being thoughtless by not inviting a section of people who should be important—the children. I say "you might be invited" because you may not make it onto future guest lists if your own wedding is seen as snooty and exclusive. By choosing to get married, a lot of people would say that you are choosing to make a public commitment and to share your love and happiness with the rest of the world. If you don't want little ones there, you can run away and get married, but you can't have it both ways.

Weddings were much simpler in Jane Austen's time—maybe you should take your cue from that. If you keep yours simple and shortish, there'll be less chance of getting too many sticky paw prints on your dress, too.

Most weddings took place in the morning. This is why Lydia Bennet is worried when her Uncle pops out on her big day—if it had got too late, they'd have had to postpone things. Weddings didn't drag on for hours and hours, the way they can now. It's no wonder that children can get bored and unruly when they have to stand about for hours in uncomfortable clothes with nothing to do and only peculiar things to eat.

After a Regency wedding, the guests would be invited for the breakfast—a very nice meal with cake—and there would be little presents for everybody. That would keep the children happy, too. You don't need to buy anything expensive—coloring books or card games would do. And try to have the party somewhere with outdoor space so that the children can run around.

Jane was adept at keeping all her nephews and nieces entertained—you should invite some people with that skill. Either pay them, or find some nice Anne Elliot to exploit. The children will bring benefits to the occasion, too. Not only can they be very entertaining, but they draw people together and give them something to talk about—particularly handy if some guests are unknown to one another.

If you really can't bear to have the children at your wedding reception, have two events; the first one could be a swift Regency-style daytime gathering with cake and small presents for the little guests; the second one could be resolutely in the evening with dancing and drinking and only adults.

On every formal visit a child ought to be of the party, by way of provision for discourse. In the present case it took up ten minutes to determine whether the boy were most like his father or mother, and in what particular he resembled either; for of course every body differed, and every body was astonished at the opinion of the others.

SENSE AND SENSIBILITY

WHAT IF MY FAMILY EMBARRASSES ME IN FRONT OF MY FIANCÉ'S RELATIVES?

YOU'VE JUST ACCEPTED YOUR BOYFRIEND'S MARRIAGE PROPOSAL AND YOU CAN'T WAIT TO TELL THE WORLD ... AND TO SHOW OFF YOUR SHINY NEW RING, OF COURSE. THE TWO OF YOU ARE PLANNING A BIG ENGAGEMENT PARTY TO BREAK THE GOOD NEWS, BUT THERE'S ONE PROBLEM: A COUPLE OF YOUR RELATIVES ARE SOCIALLY CHALLENGED, TO PUT IT KINDLY, AND YOU DON'T WANT THEM TO SCARE OFF YOUR MAN OR YOUR PROSPECTIVE IN-LAWS. IS THERE A POLITE WAY NOT TO INVITE THEM OR IS PUBLIC HUMILIATION INEVITABLE?

This depends on the kind of party you are planning. If the aim is to dazzle (with your sparkly new ring or your family), then go ahead, have a smaller party and invite only the people that you want to show off to and about. But if your party is about celebrating this exciting and wonderful new phase of your lives, you might as well have a big party, invite everybody, and get it over with. And remember: This might be one of only a few occasions where you and your man's clan will have a chance to mingle. There'll be this engagement party, your wedding, and then perhaps a couple of christenings and a birthday party or two, but they might not all meet again for decades! It might also be best for everybody to meet before the actual wedding—that way you can get it over with and stop worrying. Let any snooty future in-laws do their worst now.

Caroline Bingley and her sister, Louisa,
have plenty to say about Jane and Lizzy's relatives:

"I have an excessive regard for Jane Bennet; she is really a very sweet girl, and I wish with all my heart she were well settled. But with such a father and mother, and such low connections, I am afraid there is no chance of it."

"I think I have heard you say that their uncle is an attorney in Meryton."

"Yes; and they have another, who lives somewhere near Cheapside."

"That is capital," added her sister, and they both laughed heartily.

"If they had uncles enough to fill all Cheapside," cried Bingley, "it would not make them one jot less agreeable."

"But it must very materially lessen their chance of marrying men of any consideration in the world," replied Darcy.

To this speech Bingley made no answer; but his sisters gave it their hearty assent, and indulged their mirth for some time at the expense of their dear friend's vulgar relations.

PRIDE AND PREJUDICE

Also keep in mind that other people might not see your relatives in the same way you do. Take *Sense and Sensibility*'s Mrs. Jennings. One person might encounter her at a cocktail party and find her simply "vulgar"; another might appreciate her friendly demeanor.

Relatives are something like teeth; not many people have a perfect set. Even Miss Bingley, who was so snobby about the Bennets, was conveniently forgetting that her own antecedents had been in trade. Her brother was only renting that house in the country—they weren't of the gentry yet—so were actually lower down the social scale than Jane and Lizzy. Nobody sensible would have wanted to ask that arch snob, Lady Catherine, to a party. Lady Catherine is one of the most "socially challenged" of all Jane Austen's characters. Remember all the perfectly vile things she says to Lizzy? Jane makes it very clear that just being rich does not mean someone will be nicely behaved.

Elizabeth Bennet found her mother's behavior excruciating, and her younger sisters (including Mary) were always embarrassing her in public, but Mr. Darcy fell for her anyway. It was when Lydia brought potential disgrace and social ostracism on the Bennets that Mr. Darcy finally showed how much he really loved Lizzy. And she put up with Lady Catherine for his sake—it is actually Lizzy who persuades him to carry on being kind to her after the wedding. It works both ways; you probably haven't met all of your beloved's family yet. He may have Mrs. Elton or Mr. Palmer waiting in the wings. It's best to let everybody meet now—that way you can leave yourself more time to tackle the dreaded seating plan.

> *With the Gardiners they were always on the most intimate terms. Darcy, as well as Elizabeth, really loved them; and they were both ever sensible of the warmest gratitude toward the persons who, by bringing her into Derbyshire, had been the means of uniting them.*
>
> PRIDE AND PREJUDICE

This isn't just a *Pride and Prejudice* scenario: Captain Wentworth puts up with the appalling Sir Walter Elliot; Elinor Dashwood puts up with her plotting sister-in-law, as well as with Edward's horrible mother and silly brother; Mr. Knightley is happy to move in to Hartfield so that Emma can continue to look after her high-maintenance father; and Catherine Morland will put up with the horrible General Tilney. The list goes on and on ...

If your fiancé really loves you, he will do so whatever your relatives are like. Are you worried that his love won't survive the engagement party? Well, you'll have to weather far worse storms than this if the marriage is going to work. Once you have got through the unavoidable few gatherings necessary, you can engineer ways of spending time with those relatives that you really like. When you and your boyfriend get married, you'll be uniting two families and starting a new one of your own. Mr. and Mrs. Darcy can choose whom to invite to Pemberley, and you can do likewise, although you won't always be able to control who turns up unannounced: "Mr. Bennet missed his second daughter exceedingly; his affection for her drew him oftener from home than anything else could do. He delighted in going to Pemberley, especially when he was least expected." *

Lady Catherine was extremely indignant on the marriage of her nephew; and as she gave way to all the genuine frankness of her character, in her reply to the letter which announced its arrangement, she sent him language so very abusive, especially of Elizabeth, that for some time all intercourse was at an end. But at length, by Elizabeth's persuasion, he was prevailed on to overlook the offense, and seek a reconciliation …

PRIDE AND PREJUDICE

HOW DO I SAY GOOD-BYE TO A FAIR-WEATHER FRIEND?

Q WE ALL SEEM TO HAVE THAT ONE FRIEND: SHE NEVER CALLS, ASKS YOU ON A NIGHT OUT, OR EVEN ASKS YOU ABOUT YOURSELF ANYMORE UNLESS SHE WANTS SOMETHING. IN FACT, YOU CAN'T REMEMBER THE LAST TIME THE TWO OF YOU HAD A GOOD CHAT AS FRIENDS—EVERY MEETING WITH HER TURNS INTO AN EXERCISE IN SELF-LOATHING AFTER YOU ONCE AGAIN AGREE TO HELP HER AGAINST YOUR BETTER JUDG-MENT. YOU'RE TORN BETWEEN FEELING THAT THE FRIENDSHIP IS OVER AND ENOUGH IS ENOUGH, AND NOT KNOWING HOW TO SAY NO BECAUSE YOU STILL REMEMBER THE GOOD TIMES. HOW CAN YOU PUT YOUR FOOT DOWN ONCE AND FOR ALL?

> *I have lost a treasure, such a sister, such a friend as never can have been surpassed. She was the sun of my life, the gilder of every pleasure, the soother of every sorrow; I had not a thought concealed from her, and it is as if I had lost a part of myself.*
>
> LETTER FROM
> CASSANDRA AUSTEN TO
> FANNY KNIGHT ON THE DEATH
> OF JANE, WINCHESTER,
> JULY 20TH, 1817

A Cassandra was probably Jane Austen's most steadfast friend, and that relationship seems to have sustained her and acted as a buffer against undesirable acquaintances. She had other good friends, too; Martha Lloyd (who came to live with them at Chawton), Catherine and Alethea Bigg, and Anne Sharp, the governess to her brother Edward's children, were among those most important to her. She seems to have been discerning in choosing her friends. It's notable that Anne Sharp, rather than any of the rich relatives or neighbors, is the person whose company Jane found most congenial when she was staying at Godmersham, Edward's grand home in Kent. Anne, who like Jane was an intelligent, resourceful, working woman, became "My Dearest Anne." Jane corresponded affectionately with her, invited her to stay, and sent her copies of her books. When Jane died, Cassandra, knowing the importance of the friendship, sent Anne Sharp a lock of her sister's hair and a few little keepsakes.

So Jane was canny in choosing her friends and clever enough to avoid entanglements with false ones. She loved a few people faithfully. However, her spells away at school and those many hours spent at balls, visiting neighbors, and in society must have given her ample opportunity to observe the people that she *didn't* want to be friends with. With her sharp tongue, and the focus and determination that any artist needs to succeed at her work, some people may have chosen not to be friends with her too!

Jane would advise you to extricate yourself from this relationship. She didn't waste time and affection on the undeserving, and nor should you. Her work gives us many examples of undesirable friends and what these entanglements can bring.

Lucy Steele in *Sense and Sensibility* singles out Elinor Dashwood and decides that they are to be the best of friends. Lucy's wheedling ways are all part of her plan to keep Edward Ferrars ensnared. Elinor is polite and behaves impeccably, but she is never the one to seek Lucy out and does nothing to nourish the friendship. Once Lucy's gold-digging plans have finally worked and she's settled in London, we can rest assured that she won't bother herself with Elinor.

Be like Elinor, polite but chilly. Do nothing to further or extend the friendship. Jane Austen doesn't mention any further interaction between Lucy and Elinor after their weddings, and I'm certain that Elinor would have tried to avoid any invitations to stay with her in London, if they had been made. You must do likewise.

Isabella Thorpe in *Northanger Abbey* is of similar character to Lucy. She tries to manipulate the innocent Catherine Morland, professing love for Catherine's brother, James, until a better prospect seems to come along. She is no friend to Catherine and continually puts her in awkward situations. Catherine is only seventeen and it takes her a while and a little help to realize what Isabella is really like. Eventually, she receives a last, cajoling letter from Isabella. It is the final straw: "Such a strain of shallow artifice could not impose even upon Catherine. Its inconsistencies, contradictions, and falsehood struck her from the very first. She was ashamed of Isabella, and ashamed of having ever loved her. Her professions of attachment were now as disgusting as her excuses were empty, and her demands impudent … She resolved on not answering Isabella's letter, and tried to think no more of it." *

Catherine Morland wakes up:

"So much for Isabella," she cried, "and for all our intimacy!
She must think me an idiot … but perhaps this has served to make her
character better known to me than mine is to her. I see what she has been
about. She is a vain coquette, and her tricks have not answered.
I do not believe she had ever any regard either for James or for me,
and I wish I had never known her."
"It will soon be as if you never had," said Henry.

NORTHANGER ABBEY

You must do the same. It won't be easy—you may be met with some resistance from your friend, who is used to getting her own way—but a time comes when some friendships simply must be ended.

Fanny Price, a shrewder judge of character than Catherine, has a similar problem with the glamorous Mary Crawford. Mary is amoral, clever, and selfish, but she is sometimes kind to Fanny. Even when Mary offers to come and rescue Fanny from exile in Portsmouth, Fanny stands firm: "She thanked Miss Crawford, but gave a decided negative." †

You must be just as frosty and just as firm. Don't be tempted by seemingly kind offers or appeals to old times. If Fanny and Catherine can do it, so can you.

* *NA*, Ch27. † *MP*, Ch45

WORK & CAREER

THERE'S PLENTY OF ADVICE HERE TO HELP
YOU DEAL WITH PROBLEMS IN THE MODERN
WORKFORCE. DESPITE BEING A GEORGIAN
GENTLEMAN'S DAUGHTER, JANE AUSTEN HAD
A SUCCESSFUL CAREER AND MANAGED
TO JUGGLE WRITING WITH FAMILY
RESPONSIBILITIES AND SOCIAL DUTIES. WHAT
SHE HAS TO SAY ABOUT HANDLING TRICKY
SITUATIONS AND IMPOSSIBLE PEOPLE IS AS
RELEVANT NOW AS IT WAS THEN.

IS IT BETTER TO FOLLOW MY DREAMS
OR GET A REAL JOB?

YOU'VE NEVER BEEN INTERESTED IN WALKING THE BEATEN PATH. WHILE YOUR PARENTS WOULD PREFER IT IF YOU WENT TO LAW SCHOOL OR BECAME A DOCTOR, YOU'RE DETERMINED TO BE A WRITER. FRIENDS AND FAMILY ALL WARN YOU OF THE INSTABILITY OF THE WRITER'S LIFESTYLE AND CLAIM TO BE LOOKING OUT FOR YOUR BEST INTERESTS—YOU UNDERSTAND THEIR PERSPECTIVE, BUT YOU DON'T WANT TO END UP TRAPPED IN A JOB YOU HATE. IS IT A BAD IDEA TO IGNORE REALITY IN THE PURSUIT OF HAPPINESS?

> *People are more ready to borrow and praise than to buy, which*
> *I cannot wonder at; but though I like praise as well as anybody,*
> *I like what Edward calls "Pewter," too.*
>
> LETTER TO FANNY KNIGHT, LONDON, NOVEMBER 30TH, 1814

Your friends and family are right to warn you. Writers are rarely rich and the rents on Parisian garrets now cost a lot of what Edward (Jane Austen's rich brother) called "pewter." You may think that you don't care about money, but it will be a different matter when, in a few years' time, you're scrabbling around in the bottom of your thrift shop bag, trying to find the bus fare. Many writers are other things, too—not many can survive on their writing income alone. The situation is the same now as it was in 1814, when Jane was confiding in her niece. Writers' incomes are unreliable and readers are more likely to borrow books than to buy them. And, unfortunately, critics' praise is no guarantee of sales.

Jane would advise you to work hard and be practical if you want those dreams to come true. There's debate about precisely when Jane began her earlier works, but we know that there were around seventeen years between the first composition of *Sense and Sensibility* and *Pride and Prejudice* and their respective publication dates. It was only after *Sense and Sensibility* and *Pride and Prejudice* had been published and well received that Jane's work rate speeded up.

During her last months, Jane gave advice to her nieces and nephews who wanted to follow in her footsteps. Caroline Austen recalled: "As I grew older, she would talk to me more seriously of my reading and my amusements. I had taken early to writing verses and stories, and I am sorry to think how I troubled her with reading them. She was very kind about it, and always had some praise to bestow, but at last she warned me against spending too much time upon them. She said— how well I recollect it!—that she knew writing stories was a great amusement, and she thought a harmless one, though many people, she was aware, thought other-wise; but that at my age it would be bad for me to be much taken up with my own compositions. Later still—it was after she had gone to Winchester—she sent me a message to this effect, that if I would take her advice I should cease writing till I was sixteen; that she had herself often wished she had read more, and written less in the corresponding years of her own life." *

I think Jane would advise you in the same way: read. And remember that nobody likes being poor.

* From Caroline Austen's *My Aunt Jane Austen: A Memoir* (1867) included in Austen-Leigh, J.E., ed. Sutherland, K. (2008)

HOW CAN I GET MY TWENTY-SOMETHING TO GROW UP?

Q YOUR DAUGHTER HAS JUST GRADUATED FROM COLLEGE AND IT'S TIME FOR HER TO STRIKE OUT ON HER OWN. UNFORTUNATELY, FROM YOUR PERSPECTIVE, SHE STILL HASN'T LEFT THE CHILD MENTALITY BEHIND. SHE ACTS MORE LIKE A THOUGHTLESS TEENAGER THAN A POTENTIAL CAREER WOMAN, WHICH LEAVES YOU DESPAIRING OF HER ABILITY TO FIND GAINFUL EMPLOYMENT (AND EVENTUALLY MOVE OUT OF THE HOUSE!). IS THERE ANY WAY YOU CAN GIVE HER A SHOVE IN THE DIRECTION OF ADULTHOOD AND RESPONSIBILITY?

A Mrs. Austen would sympathize with you. She must have despaired of Jane and wondered what would become of her. In 1796, she wrote to one of her future daughters-in-law: "I look forward to you as a real comfort to me in my old age, when Cassandra has gone to Shropshire, and Jane—the Lord knows where ..."*

Mrs. Austen must have felt as though her children were all settled, apart from Jane. Cassandra's future in Shropshire disappeared when her fiancé died, so she had a good excuse to stay at home; it was as though she became

* Letter from Mrs. Austen to Mary Lloyd, November 30th, 1796 in Austen-Leigh, W. and Austen-Leigh, R., revised and enlarged by Le Faye, D. (1989).

> *This scheme was that she should accompany her brother back to Portsmouth, and spend a little time with her own family ... his prime motive in sending her away had very little to do with the propriety of her seeing her parents again, and nothing at all with any idea of making her happy ... a little abstinence from the elegancies and luxuries of Mansfield Park would bring her mind into a sober state, and incline her to a juster estimate of the value of that home of greater permanence, and equal comfort, of which she had the offer ... Poor Fanny!*
>
> MANSFIELD PARK

a widow. Cassandra had a small legacy from Tom Fowle. Jane had only what her family could give her, and that was very little. What was to become of Jane?

Cassandra took on responsibility for running the household; Jane's main task was to get up early to make tea and play the piano—something she probably wanted to do anyway! When Cassandra was away and Jane took over, we have a sense that although she did it well enough, she was only playing at housekeeping. She wrote to Cassandra: "My mother desires me to tell you that I am a very good housekeeper, which I have no reluctance in doing, because I really think it my peculiar excellence, and for this reason—I always take care to provide such things as please my own appetite, which I consider as the chief merit in housekeeping." *

She can't help but poke fun at whatever task she is given as a way of coping with the tedium of much of it. Perhaps she was also feeling dreadfully bored and depressed. Cassandra was away at Godmersham, their brother's swanky house in Kent, while she was stuck at home with their mother.

* Letter to Cassandra, Steventon, November 17th, 1798

But Jane liked home comforts as much as anybody. When she is away in London, she begins a letter that will contain important news of publishing deals and their brother Henry's illness like this:

"Hans Place, Tuesday Oct: 17. [1815]

My dear Cassandra

Thank you for your two Letters. I am very glad the new Cook begins so well. Good apple pies are a considerable part of our domestic happiness. –Mr. Murray's Letter is come; he is a Rogue of course, but a civil one. He offers £450—but wants to have the Copyright of MP & S&S included . . ."

Although Jane, Cassandra, and their mother lived relatively simply, they still had a cook and servants. It sounds as though your daughter has, too. She needs to be expected to do more than make tea and play the piano.

In December 1794, Jane's father bought her a beautiful writing box— a portable desk with a slope and drawers for papers and pens. It's in the British Library today. We can guess that it was a birthday present and that with this gift came an acknowledgment of her talent. You should help your daughter find out what her talent is and actively encourage her in that direction. Give her the mental equivalent of the portable desk and tell her to get on and use it.

Perhaps your daughter is stuck in a rut and needs some help getting out of it. Kind and sensible Mrs. Gardiner senses Elizabeth's growing frustration and boredom with life at home and the Meryton marriage market. She offers to take Elizabeth with her on a tour of the Lake District. Elizabeth really does need to get away; this offer will change her life. You won't want to give your daughter an extended vacation, but perhaps she needs to get away, too. Most people need a little help in the right direction, or to be given a way out sometimes.

Sir Thomas Bertram is another frustrated (proxy) parent. Fanny Price would be happy to stay at Mansfield Park forever and she certainly doesn't want to marry Henry Crawford. Sir Thomas decides upon a plan to force Fanny into activity; he sends her to stay with her parents in their horribly inferior house in Portsmouth, so she can experience life without the benefit of so many luxuries.

If your daughter doesn't respond to an upping of domestic responsibilities or you giving her a psychological writing slant, you must do what Sir Thomas did—send her to Portsmouth.

She had the unexpected happiness of an invitation to accompany her uncle and aunt in a tour of pleasure which they proposed taking in the summer. "We have not quite determined how far it shall carry us," said Mrs. Gardiner, "but, perhaps, to the Lakes." No scheme could have been more agreeable to Elizabeth, and her acceptance of the invitation was most ready and grateful. "My dear, dear aunt," she rapturously cried, "what delight! what felicity! You give me fresh life and vigor. Adieu to disappointment and spleen. What are men to rocks and mountains?"

PRIDE AND PREJUDICE

HOW DO YOU BALANCE CHILDREN AND A CAREER?

YOU'VE MADE IT TO YOUR THIRTIES IN ONE PIECE, AND NOW YOU WANT TO START A FAMILY. WHILE YOU CAN'T WAIT TO BECOME A MOTHER—YOU'VE WANTED KIDS FOR YEARS—YOU HAVE COME TO REALIZE THAT YOU WANT TO CONTINUE IN YOUR CAREER AS WELL. OF COURSE, YOU'RE WORRIED THAT IF YOU TRY TO HAVE A CAREER AND CHILDREN, YOU'LL END UP OVERSTRETCHED, UNSATISFIED, AND FEELING LIKE YOU'RE NEGLECTING EITHER YOUR JOB OR YOUR FAMILY. IS THERE A WAY TO MAKE IT WORK?

Jane Austen didn't have children of her own, but she certainly spent plenty of time looking after other people's. The Austens were a huge family, and Jane's brothers had dozens. As well as looking after their mother, Jane and Cassandra were constantly in demand as aunts. There were streams of visitors to their Chawton cottage, and when they weren't being visited, they were likely to be doing the visiting. That Jane ever got anything finished is impressive.

It's lucky for us that Jane didn't have children (death in childbirth was a huge risk). She loved being an aunt, but must sometimes have longed for everybody to leave her alone so that she could work. She would have had little control over who was suddenly coming to stay, and who

I was not sorry when Friday came. It had been a busy week, and I wanted a few days quiet and exemption from the thought and contrivancy which any sort of company gives ... I often wonder how you can find time for what you do, in addition to the care of the house; and how good Mrs. West could have written such books and collected so many hard works, with all her family cares, is still more a matter of astonishment. Composition seems to me impossible with a head full of joints of mutton and doses of rhubarb.

LETTER TO CASSANDRA, CHAWTON, SEPTEMBER 8TH, 1816

wanted their sister-in-law to help when a new baby arrived. If Cassandra was the one going away, Jane would have had added burdens at home. There was often no escape.

Jane acknowledged that there would be times when work would be impossible, and there were other periods of her life when we don't know what, if anything, she was working on. I find it hard to believe that she could ever have stopped writing entirely; even during her least productive years in Bath, she may have been revising her earlier novels. Of course, being a writer isn't the same as having a regular job, but if one wants to get anything done, one has to act as though it is.

It's easy to make plans before a baby arrives and, although you can't know how you'll feel and how demanding each child will be, there's no harm in starting out with a game plan. Jane took her work seriously and made sure that other people did, too. It wasn't "Jane's little hobby." Even before she was published, her ambition and dedication to her craft were apparent to those closest to her. Her attitude was always that "an artist cannot do anything slovenly." * She could make jokes about her work, but underneath she was always completely serious.

* Letter to Cassandra, Steventon, November 17th, 1798

Jane carved out space for herself. She got up before the rest of the household so that she could be alone, and she walked, keeping her own handmade notebooks in her pockets. Cassandra took on the majority of the household management. Take a tip from Jane and accept help. Apart from the small matter of her genius, it was dedication, hard work, being organized, and valuing what she did that helped her write those wonderful novels.

Jane wondered how "good Mrs. West" managed to write her novels (these included *A Gossip's Story* and *The Advantages of Education*, both published in the 1790s and probable sources of inspiration for *Sense and Sensibility*). Nowadays, Jane wouldn't have to be so isolated; she'd be able to find out how other women did it and establish networks. You should do the same.

Jane needed to switch between the different aspects of her life and to not only be able to put down her pen when family duties called, but to pick it up and get on with her work right away as soon she was alone.

"No, indeed," she wrote to Cassandra, "I am never too busy to think of *Sense and Sensibility*. I can no more forget it than a mother can forget her sucking child; and I am much obliged to you for your inquiries. I have had two sheets to correct, but the last only brings us to Willoughby's first appearance." *

Jane enjoyed all aspects of her life when she wasn't working—don't see these possible children as items on your To-Do list. The letters and recollections of Jane's nephews and nieces paint a picture of an aunt who loved to spend time with them, playing games, telling stories, going boating, and inspiring several of them to write, too. She wasn't somebody who batted them away. If children arrive, Jane would tell you to make sure that you enjoy being with them.

Of course, Jane did have her own particular kind of children: her novels. Having penned so many letters about other people's babies, it must have been with real delight that her letter announcing the safe delivery of *Pride and Prejudice* was sent and received.

> *I want to tell you that I have got my own darling child from London.*
> *On Wednesday I received one copy sent down by Falkener, with three lines*
> *from Henry to say that he had given another to Charles and sent a third by*
> *the coach to Godmersham ... I must confess that I think her [Elizabeth] as*
> *delightful a creature as ever appeared in print ...*
>
> LETTER TO CASSANDRA, CHAWTON, JANUARY 29TH, 1813

* Letter to Cassandra, London, April 25th, 1811

HOW CAN I MAKE TIME FOR THE GYM
ON MY TO-DO LIST?

 YOU LOVE YOUR WORK, BUT IT'S ONE OF THOSE JOBS THAT REQUIRES LONG HOURS, AND YOU OFTEN FEEL EXHAUSTED AND UNMOTIVATED WHEN YOU'RE OUT OF THE OFFICE. BECAUSE OF THIS, YOU HAVEN'T BEEN TAKING CARE OF YOURSELF AS WELL AS YOU COULD. NOW YOU HAVE AN IMPORTANT FUNCTION COMING UP AND YOU DESPERATELY WANT TO LOSE WEIGHT AND GET IN BETTER SHAPE SO YOU CAN FEEL COMFORTABLE WEARING A FABULOUS DRESS. HOW CAN YOU FIT EXERCISE INTO YOUR CAREER-DRIVEN LIFESTYLE?

> *We walked to Weston one evening last week, and liked it very much.*
> *Liked what very much? Weston? No, walking to Weston. I have not*
> *expressed myself properly, but I hope you will understand me.*
> LETTER TO CASSANDRA, BATH, JUNE 11TH, 1799

There were many demands on Jane Austen's time. She had to lead the life of a Georgian lady with the constant rounds of visits, help to run the household (particularly when Cassandra was away), spend endless days with her nephews and nieces, help her sisters-in-law whenever one of them had a baby (and that was often), look after her mother, dash off endless letters, and, in between all of this, write those wonderful novels. She even made her own little notebooks.

Jane kept herself fit and sane by dint of a good diet and plenty of exercise. By walking, she was able to escape from other people, and I suspect that much of her work in plotting and planning was done outdoors. Sometimes she walked by herself and sometimes with friends or family. She described herself and her friend Martha as "desperate walkers"; only the most appalling stormy weather could keep them indoors. Become a desperate walker. Jane's heroines love to walk, and they walk a long way, fitting this exercise into their routines whenever they can.

I wouldn't recommend a Georgian diet, or at least not the kind that the rich enjoyed. The Prince Regent's fat stomach was said to hit the floor when he was out of his stays; but you could follow their lead and try to drink more tea and eat a lot more fresh fruit. The Austens had apples, apricots, asparagus, cherries, currants, gooseberries, plums, pears, mulberries, raspberries, strawberries … and those are just things that Jane happened to mention in her letters.

Tea (from China) was extremely popular and considered an absolute necessity, but "tea" made from other things was drunk, too. A dandelion tea, such as Mrs. Austen drank for her many bilious (and Jane might have thought spurious) complaints, might help you.

Another Georgian solution could help you to relax as well as look and feel better—visit a spa. Being pummeled and pampered might make the world of difference. Are you really too busy for just one Saturday or Sunday afternoon off?

Start planning what to wear now. A cleverly cut dress, flowing and designed to flatter in just the way that Regency dresses did, will cover a multitude of sins.

If more drastic measures are called for, try the Mr. Woodhouse program: "'You must go to bed early, my dear—and I recommend a little gruel to you before you go. You and I will have a nice basin of gruel together. My dear Emma, suppose we all have a little gruel.' Emma could not suppose any such thing …"*

*E, Ch12

SHOULD I USE MY OFFICE POWER FOR GOOD OR EVIL?

Q THE TASK OF COORDINATING THE TRANSPORT FOR THE OFFICE ANNUAL PICNIC HAS FALLEN TO YOU. WHILE ORGANIZING CAR POOLS TO THE EVENT, YOU HAD AN IDEA THAT WOULD UNDOUBTEDLY BE POPULAR BUT ALSO MORALLY DUBIOUS: THERE ARE A COUPLE OF BORING PEOPLE IN YOUR OFFICE WITH WHOM NO ONE IS EAGER TO SOCIALIZE, AND—IF YOU WERE SO INCLINED—YOU COULD MAKE IT VERY DIFFICULT FOR THEM TO GET TO THE PICNIC, AND EVEN GIVE THEM A HEAVY HINT THAT THEY WOULDN'T BE MISSED. SHOULD YOU ACT FOR THE GREATER GOOD OF THE PARTY OR BE THE BETTER PERSON?

> "Emma..., I cannot see you acting wrong, without a remonstrance. How could you be so unfeeling to Miss Bates? How could you be so insolent in your wit to a woman of her character, age, and situation? Emma, I had not thought it possible... Her situation should secure your compassion. It was badly done, indeed."
>
> EMMA

 Tut, tut. You'd better do what you know to be right or you'll get a very stern telling off from Mr. Knightley, and not only that, you'll feel terrible and almost everybody will think badly of you. This is the office annual picnic, not a private party of yours. If you'd like to organize one of those, go ahead, but this is meant to be for everyone. It would be dreadfully wrong of you to exclude or be rude to these people, even if they are boring.

Jane Austen shows what a true hero Mr. Knightley is by the way that he takes care of other people. He doesn't just reprove Emma for being rude to Miss Bates, he goes out of his way to make sure that his needier neighbors are treated well. He never makes a show of his good deeds. At the Coles' party, Mrs. Weston, Emma's kindly ex-governess, discovers that she is already too late to offer transport to Miss Bates and Jane Fairfax; Mr. Knightley has got there first: "'Good soul! she was 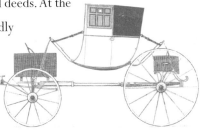 as grateful as possible, you may be sure. "Nobody was ever so fortunate as herself!"—but with many, many thanks,—"there was no occasion to trouble us, for Mr. Knightley's carriage had brought, and was to take them home again."'" *

Emma has a lot to learn about human relationships. While she just wants to be the queen of local society, other people are busy trying to bring others together for fun. She is slowly learning how she should behave. She just about manages to keep quiet when amiable Mr. Weston tells her about a plan for a day out, a plan that the appalling Mrs. Elton will be able to claim as her own: "'I am glad you approve of what I have done,' said he very comfortably. 'But I thought you would. Such schemes as these are nothing without numbers. One cannot have too large a party. A large party secures its own amusement. And she is a good-natured woman after all. One could not leave her out.'" †

Mr. Weston is right about large gatherings—if you have everybody there it will be more of a party—it just wouldn't be the annual office picnic without them all. Not only must Miss Bates and Mrs. Elton be included, but you'd better be nice to them. This is what Emma has to learn. See how nice Mr. and Mrs. Weston and kind Mr. Knightley behave. They should be your models here.

* E, Ch26. † E, Ch42

IS THERE SUCH A THING AS "WOMEN'S WORK" ANYMORE?

YOU AND YOUR PARTNER ARE THE DEFINITION OF A MODERN COUPLE: YOU BOTH WORK AND CONTRIBUTE FINANCIALLY TO THE MORTGAGE AND HOUSEHOLD. BUT THAT'S AS FAR AS THE EQUALITY GOES. HE SEEMS TO THINK THAT THE UPKEEP OF THE HOUSE IS YOUR DOMAIN. HE'S NEVER COME OUT AND SAID IT, BUT YOU SUSPECT HE THINKS THAT HOUSEWORK IS "WOMEN'S WORK" AND THAT YOUR JOB IS MORE A HOBBY THAN A CAREER. HOW CAN YOU MAKE HIM SEE THE LIGHT OF EQUALITY AND GET HIM TO DO MORE THAN WASH A DISH OR TWO EVERY ONCE IN A WHILE?

If only you had ascertained what this man's attitudes were before you set up home with him! The Georgian solution to your problem requires a large disposable income. Paid staff is what you need—that way, neither of you will have to do much at all. Even a family as down at heel as the Prices in *Mansfield Park* had servants, including the unsatisfactory and "trollopy-looking" Rebecca. However, who could blame her for being that way when she had to wait on them?

The Austens always had servants; even in a home as modest as their Chawton cottage they employed a few. Today, many couples try to achieve domestic harmony by paying somebody else to do some of the work, but an unfair share is still often left to one partner, usually the woman. If men have always had things done for them, they just won't appreciate all there is that needs doing. It was ever thus—here is Jane writing to Cassandra about the number of servants they want to have when they move to Bath. Their father is retiring, and the women of the house are plotting behind his back. It seems Mr. and Mrs. Austen had differing ideas about the amount of work involved in running a household.

"My mother looks forward with as much certainty as you can do to our keeping two maids; my father is the only one not in the secret. We plan having a steady cook and a young, giddy housemaid, with a sedate, middle-aged man, who is to undertake the double office of husband to the former and sweetheart to the latter. No children, of course, to be allowed on either side." *

> Mary Musgrove complains to Anne Elliot:
> *"If there is anything disagreeable going on, men are always sure to get out of it, and Charles is as bad as any of them ... So here he is to go away and enjoy himself, and because I am the poor mother, I am not to be allowed to stir ... I am not at all equal to it."*
> PERSUASION

In the end, employing a cleaner for a couple of hours a week may take the edge off your seething resentment, but it won't actually change your partner's attitude. And things will only get much worse if children come along.

In *Persuasion*, Mary Musgrove complains to her sister Anne Elliot about men because she wants to go out, too; eventually she does, leaving poor Anne to babysit. Jane tells us that Mary Musgrove said nothing until "there was only Anne to hear," and that was her mistake. There is no point in complaining when your partner is not around. Unless you want to take on some servants or have a kind sister like Anne to exploit, Jane's advice would be to talk to this man about how you feel.

* Letter to Cassandra, Steventon, January 3rd, 1801

HOW CAN I DEAL WITH AN OFFICE DRAGON?

YOU LOVE YOUR JOB. THE WORK, THE PEOPLE, THE OFFICE—ALL MAKE YOU ALMOST HAPPY TO HEAR THAT ALARM SOUND IN THE MORNING. HOWEVER, THERE'S ONE OFFICE FIXTURE INTENT ON RUINING YOUR HAPPINESS—A BOSS FROM ANOTHER DEPARTMENT. SHE'S BEEN WORKING THERE LONGER THAN ANYONE CAN REMEMBER AND, DESPITE THE FACT THAT YOU DON'T REPORT TO HER, SHE STILL THINKS SHE HAS THE RIGHT TO STICK HER NOSE IN AND CRITICIZE WHAT YOU DO. YOU'VE AVOIDED CONFRONTATION BECAUSE THERE'S A POSSIBLE PROMOTION ON THE HORIZON, BUT YOU'RE TIRED OF HER COMMENTS AND YOUR BITTEN TONGUE WILL SOON BEGIN TO BLEED. HOW CAN YOU SLAY THE DRAGON WITHOUT A FULLY FLEDGED BATTLE?

Your dragon sounds something like Mrs. Norris, evil aunt and bully of Fanny Price. From the moment Fanny arrives at Mansfield Park, Mrs. Norris is determined that Fanny will be kept at the very bottom of the pecking order. Perhaps there's a part of Mrs. Norris that realizes that her own position is not that different from Fanny's—they are both poor relations and there on sufferance.

Mrs. Norris makes a point of belittling Fanny, giving her endless unpleasant little tasks and constantly reminding her of how grateful she should feel. It's difficult for meek little Fanny to strike back; the war has to be won in different ways, but eventually it is. Perhaps your interfering office dragon feels her own position is being made insecure by you or that you are somehow showing up her shortcomings.

Your boss may be too busy or distant to notice how this woman is interfering.

Mrs. Norris puts down Fanny Price:

"The nonsense and folly of people's stepping out of their rank and trying to appear above themselves, makes me think it right to give you a hint ... I do beseech and entreat you not to be putting yourself forward, and talking and giving your opinion as if you were one of your cousins ... That will never do, believe me. Remember, wherever you are, you must be the lowest and last ..."

MANSFIELD PARK

It took Sir Thomas a long time to realize the poisonous effect of Mrs. Norris (his sister-in-law) but eventually he did, and she was banished. It may also take your boss a while, but eventually he or she should realize what this woman is doing and re-establish control. It probably isn't a good idea to complain to your boss about her, but you could happen to mention some of the things that she asks you to do at your next catch-up meeting. Fanny had to treat her dragon with respect, and so must you. Insubordination will only get you into trouble. Your tact and ability to keep your cool will help you on the way up the ladder. And you, like Fanny Price, will triumph in the end.

The thing that really helps get Fanny through is the affection and support of her cousin, Edmund Bertram. He is almost all that poor Fanny has, but it sounds as though there are plenty of nice people to offer you solidarity. The other thing that Fanny does is retreat to the sanctuary of her room. Don't hide in the restroom, but you may be able to occupy yourself with some highly important task elsewhere when you see this evil woman coming.

It may seem that things will never change, but they will. All dictators eventually die, retire, or are overthrown or moved to other departments; one day your Mrs. Norris will lose her power. Until then, carry on being as calm, contained, and respectful as Fanny Price, quietly believing that virtue will (at last) be rewarded and that you will prevail.

Eventually, Sir Thomas realizes how horrible Mrs. Norris is, and she has to leave Mansfield Park. Play your cards right and you will live happily ever after: "Here had been grievous mismanagement . . . It ended in Mrs. Norris's resolving to quit . . . She was regretted by no one at Mansfield. Not even Fanny had tears for Aunt Norris, not even when she was gone forever." *

That's Plan A, but it may reach a point where you simply cannot keep biting your tongue and you need to have a showdown with this woman. If this happens, remember that she is older and higher ranking than you. Fanny Price would never have stood up to Mrs. Norris like this; Elizabeth Bennet must be your model instead for Plan B.

Lady Catherine de Bourgh thinks that her whole empire is being threatened by Elizabeth, so she arrives uninvited at Longbourn, planning to subdue Lizzy once and for all. She is rude from the moment she arrives: "'That lady, I suppose, is your mother? . . . And *that*, I suppose, is one of your sisters? . . . You have a very small park here . . .'"†

MP, Ch48. † *P&P*, Ch56

That's just for starters. She refuses any refreshments and peers into rooms. Her sole intention is to intimidate Elizabeth into promising not to marry Mr. Darcy, so she gets her alone in the garden to begin the campaign in earnest. Elizabeth remains frostily polite in the face of extreme provocation, and despite being insulted and lectured, does not allow herself to be bullied.

Elizabeth Bennet stands up to Lady Catherine de Bourgh:
"I am not to be intimidated into anything so wholly unreasonable ... Allow me to say, Lady Catherine, that the arguments with which you have supported this extraordinary application have been as frivolous as the application was ill-judged. You have widely mistaken my character, if you think I can be worked on by such persuasions as these. How far your nephew might approve of your interference in his affairs, I cannot tell; but you have certainly no right to concern yourself in mine. I must beg, therefore, to be importuned no farther on the subject."

PRIDE AND PREJUDICE

When news of how she has stood up to his aunt reaches Mr. Darcy, it gives him hope that Elizabeth will one day accept his proposal. In the same way, standing up to the office bully in a calm and professional manner should speed you on your path to promotion. Perhaps other people are longing for somebody to stand up to her and will silently applaud when you do.

There is another possible way—a Plan C. Why not do what Jane did and immortalize your bullies in fiction? Think of it all as great material and just start taking notes.

I HAVE AN INTERVIEW FOR THE JOB OF MY DREAMS. HOW CAN I BE SURE TO PUT MY BEST FOOT FORWARD?

Q TO BUILD THE CAREER YOU WANT, YOU REALLY NEED TO STAND OUT FROM THE CROWD, PARTICULARLY WHEN IT COMES TO APPLYING FOR JOBS. HOWEVER, IT'S DIFFICULT TO ANTICIPATE WHAT SPECIAL QUALITIES AN EMPLOYER PREFERS. FOR INSTANCE, DO THEY WANT TO KNOW ABOUT YOUR INTERESTS OR JUST YOUR WORK HISTORY? IS IT MORE ATTRACTIVE TO OUTLINE YOUR ACTIVITIES OUTSIDE WORK, SUCH AS VOLUNTEERING AND RELEVANT HOBBIES, OR SHOULD YOU STICK TO THE BASICS? IS THERE SOME KIND OF MAGIC MIXTURE OF INFORMATION THAT GUARANTEES YOU'LL GET THE JOB?

A Sometimes it seems that whatever we do, we'll be judged wanting, and that whatever job we apply for, there are bound to be other people with far more experience and better qualifications, including an MA in Playing Tennis With The Boss. It's easy to feel that we'll never be noticed, or that we'll always be the unsuccessful candidate.

The fact that proper education and fulfilling employment were just not possibilities for women of Jane Austen's era makes her achievements as a novelist even more impressive. Jane and Cassandra had a few years at school, but most of their education came from their clever and well-read parents. The Austens always had plenty to read, owned plenty of books, and joined libraries wherever they were living or staying. For women, a secure future often depended on marrying well, and this required an impressive résumé of accomplishments along with a financial settlement from one's family.

> *"... no one can be really esteemed accomplished who does not greatly surpass what is usually met with. A woman must have a thorough knowledge of music, singing, drawing, dancing, and the modern languages, to deserve the word; and besides all this, she must possess a certain something in her air and manner of walking, the tone of her voice, her address and expressions, or the word will be but half deserved."*
>
> PRIDE AND PREJUDICE

When Elizabeth Bennet hears Mr. Darcy and Caroline Bingley detailing what comprises a properly accomplished young woman, she says: "I am no longer surprised at your knowing only six accomplished women. I rather wonder now at your knowing *any*." *

Young women on the marriage market had constant opportunities to display their talents and the qualities that might help them to attract the right husband. Mary Bennet, the plainest and prissiest of Elizabeth's sisters, is delighted to hear herself described to Miss Bingley as "the most accomplished girl in the neighborhood," † but the reality is that nobody really wants to spend much time with her. She can play the piano and sing, but it sounds dreadful. The equivalent today would be to have all A's in her report card but no social skills, and when Mary gets a chance to show everybody just how accomplished she is by "exhibiting" during a party at Netherfield, it ends with the hateful Bingley sisters sniggering and her father uttering the immortal words: "You have delighted us long enough." ‡

I've always felt sorry for Mary—if only she could have had a proper education, an interesting job, and some friends ... Make sure that your résumé doesn't make you seem like Mary Bennet; you must list your qualifications and achievements, but employers will want to know that you can get on with people, too.

* P&P, Ch8. † P&P, Ch3. ‡ P&P, Ch18

Jane Fairfax is well educated, beautiful, elegant, and talented. Emma hates her for it: "Why she did not like Jane Fairfax might be a difficult question to answer; Mr. Knightley had once told her it was because she saw in her the really accomplished young woman, which she wanted to be thought herself ..." * Jane Fairfax is the sort of person you wouldn't want to be competing against at an interview, but not even she would be guaranteed to get the job. If it was between Emma Woodhouse and Jane Fairfax, Emma would have the advantage if they were looking for somebody animated and good at talking to people.

Emma thinks that Jane is "... so cold, so cautious! There was no getting at her real opinion. Wrapt up in a cloak of politeness, she seemed determined to hazard nothing. She was disgustingly, was suspiciously reserved." †

Who gets the job will depend on the company and position available; if it's for a trainee wedding planner, they'll probably want Emma. She can also offer some

* E, Ch20. † Ibid.

Mr. Darcy knows what will set you apart:
"... *she must yet add something more substantial, in*
the improvement of her mind by extensive reading."
PRIDE AND PREJUDICE

useful tips on how to ensure that social occasions run smoothly, organizing party games, and meeting the dietary requirements of the most particular and pernickety of guests. If they are looking for someone to join the College Board for SATs, Mary Bennet fits the bill. Elizabeth Bennet would make a good lawyer, perhaps specializing in standing up for the oppressed or protecting the local woods.

You can't be better than Jane Fairfax at being like Jane Fairfax, so concentrate on what you love doing and excel at, and make the most of that. Marianne Dashwood might pursue a musical career, while Elinor would make an excellent principal. I can see her at the helm of a large and very successful school, quite possibly all girls. She would be wise and firm, but fair. Her students might well remain unaware of the success she enjoyed as a painter. She would exhibit at a prestigious summer show every year.

Fanny Price was able to find the perfect position for herself; being the wife of a country vicar would suit her in the 21st century, too. I wonder if she'd be able to overcome her shyness and be ordained as well. It's all about making the most of your particular talents.

You can give yourself the edge by doing what Mr. Darcy says even the most accomplished woman should do—read. Read up on all aspects of the company and what they might be looking for, and keep on learning and developing. Do your homework. They won't always want Jane Fairfax—sometimes they'll want you.

HOW DO I COPE WITH JEALOUS FRIENDS?

Q YOU HAVEN'T BEEN IN YOUR JOB FOR TOO LONG, BUT FROM YOUR RECENT SUCCESSES YOU CAN SAFELY SAY YOU CHOSE THE RIGHT FIELD FOR YOUR TALENTS AND THAT YOU'RE A REAL ASSET TO YOUR ORGANIZATION. YOU'RE MOVING UP THE RANKS MUCH FASTER THAN YOUR FRIENDS, AND WHILE THEY WERE SUPPORTIVE AT FIRST, LATELY YOU'VE BEEN THE TARGET OF SNIDE COMMENTS AND PETTY JEALOUSY. YOU DON'T WANT TO LOSE YOUR FRIENDS, BUT IT'S NOT YOUR FAULT YOU'RE SUCH A RISING STAR—FRIENDS SHOULD BE SUPPORTIVE, NOT UNDERMINING. HOW CAN YOU TELL THEM TO BE LESS HOSTILE?

"One is sick of the very name of Jane Fairfax. Every letter from her is read forty times over; her compliments to all friends go round and round again; and if she does but send her aunt the pattern of a stomacher, or knit a pair of garters for her grandmother, one hears of nothing else for a month. I wish Jane Fairfax very well; but she tires me to death."

EMMA

 Jane Austen would turn her gimlet eye on you and your colleagues, and she just might sympathize with your detractors; perhaps they are hearing endless tales of how wonderful you are and how successful you're becoming and they've simply had enough. Jane was talking about fictional characters when she said: "Pictures of perfection, as you know, make me sick and wicked ...", * but that may be how your friends are feeling about you.

* Letter to Fanny Knight, Chawton, March 23rd ,1814

Everyone was always saying how lovely Jane Fairfax was; Emma found this and Jane's cool, reserved manner annoying. Perhaps you seem like something of a Jane Fairfax at the moment—a picture of perfection. Most of the fault was on Emma's side, but Jane Fairfax should have been a little friendlier. Think about the way you are behaving. Are you being a little distant and acting too superior?

Unfortunately, there could be worse reasons for your friends' behavior. You may have unwittingly turned into one of the most boastful characters of all—John Thorpe in *Northanger Abbey*. Poor Catherine Morland—it's hard for her to escape from him. Jane would suggest that you think over your recent behavior—might you have been a little like this appalling braggard?

> ### John Thorpe tries to snare Catherine Morland:
> *All the rest of his conversation, or rather talk, began and ended with himself and his own concerns. He told her of horses which he had bought for a trifle and sold for incredible sums; of racing matches, in which his judgment had infallibly foretold the winner; of shooting parties, in which he had killed more birds ... than all his companions together.*
>
> NORTHANGER ABBEY

On what must have been one of the proudest days of her life, Jane remained quiet about her achievements. Her first copy of *Pride and Prejudice* had arrived—her heart must have been singing—but she managed to spend the evening with their neighbor, Miss Benn, and had more fun in being discreet than in showing off.

"Miss Benn dined with us on the very day of the book's coming, and in the evening we fairly set at it, and read half the first vol. to her, prefacing that, having intelligence from Henry that such a work would soon appear, we had desired him to send it whenever it came out, and I believe it passed with her unsuspected. She was amused, poor soul!" *

You don't have to pretend that you're doing badly, but you don't need to go on about your successes either. Jane knew that she could safely write to Cassandra about how happy she was, but she was generally very careful about how she was perceived by other people.

* Letter to Cassandra, Chawton, January 29th, 1813

It wasn't the done thing for a country lady to be enjoying a literary career. Jane was wise enough to know that being a public figure wouldn't allow her the tranquillity in which to work and would make writing about her own world more difficult. Although she was earning money from writing, Jane would have known that she couldn't give up the day job of being a daughter, a sister, and an aunt.

Jane had watched her brothers enjoy success in different ways. She would never get to study at Oxford or sail around the world. Her brother Edward had the huge good fortune to be adopted by the Knights as their heir—how must that have felt? Jane managed to remain sanguine about it all; as Emma Watson puts it: "We must not all expect to be individually lucky … The luck of one member of a family is luck to all." *

In 1813, Madame de Staël, the celebrated writer, was in London while Jane was staying with Henry. In Henry's *Memoir of Miss Austen*, which formed the preface to the 1833 edition of *Sense and Sensibility*, he told of how "a nobleman, personally unknown to her … was desirous of her joining a literary circle at his house." Madame de Staël was to be there, too, but Jane immediately declined the invitation. Henry said that: "To her truly delicate mind such a display would have given pain instead of pleasure." I wonder; as an adult, Jane wasn't shy. Did she disapprove of Madame de Staël's lifestyle? Was she intimidated? As such a sharp observer of characters and somebody who enjoyed the theater so much, one might think she'd have wanted to be there. I suspect that she just wanted to protect her own privacy. A place in a celebrity reality TV show? No thanks.

Jane had a few very good friends, and, of course, she had Cassandra. She made sure that those dearest to her knew that they were and she clearly valued their opinions on her work. Be discreet as Jane, and make sure that those people you care about still know it—the Martha Lloyds and Cassandra Austens will stand by you.

* *W*, Part 1

DOES BEING FORMAL JUST MAKE ME LOOK OUT OF TOUCH?

YOU'VE JUST GONE BACK TO WORK AFTER YEARS OF BEING A FULL-TIME MOM AND, IN THE LAST FIVE YEARS, SO MUCH HAS CHANGED. SOMETIMES YOU'RE APPALLED AT THE WAY A COLLEAGUE WRITES AND SIGNS OFF E-MAILS. SHE'S NEVER BEEN AWAY, SO YOU'RE PROBABLY THE ONE OUT OF STEP. SHOULD YOU ADOPT HER CASUAL STYLE OR STICK WITH THE OLD-FASHIONED WAYS? DO YOU HAVE TO PUT KISSES TO COLLEAGUES OR BE THOUGHT A FUDDY DUDDY? HOW CAN YOU TELL IF YOU'RE GETTING IT WRONG?

It might seem that everything has changed in the last five years, but things haven't really altered that much in the last two hundred. The same judgments about how to address people and how formal to be existed in Jane's time, too. It's still all about being the mistress of your pen (or keyboard). In 1813, Jane's little niece, the nine-year-old Louisa, must have been looking over Jane's shoulder as she was writing. Louisa asked to send her Aunt Cassandra "a hundred thousand million kisses." *

Jane loved to write letters. Today, she would probably be somebody who texted and tweeted ad infinitum. This is from a letter to Cassandra in 1801: "I have now attained the true art of letter-writing, which we are always told is to express on paper exactly what one would say to the same person by word of mouth. I have been talking to you almost as fast as I could the whole of this letter …" † She signs off, as she so often did, "Yours affectionately, J. A."

---

* Letter to Cassandra, Godmersham, September 23rd, 1813. † Letter to Cassandra, Steventon, January 3rd, 1801

To Messrs. Crosbie & Co.,

*Gentlemen,—In the spring of the year 1803 a MS. novel in two vols.,
entitled* Susan, *was sold to you by a gentleman of the name of Seymour,
and the purchase money £10 recd. at the same time. Six years have since
passed, and this work, of which I am myself the Authoress, has never to
the best of my knowledge appeared in print, tho' an early publication
was stipulated for at the time of sale. I can only account for such an
extraordinary circumstance by supposing the MS. by some carelessness to
have been lost, and if that was the case am willing to supply you with
another copy, if you are disposed to avail yourselves of it, and will engage
for no farther delay when it comes into your hands. It will not be in my
power from particular circumstances to command this copy before the month
of August, but then if you accept my proposal you may depend on receiving
it. Be so good as to send me a line in answer as soon as possible as my stay
in this place will not exceed a few days. Should no notice be taken of this
address, I shall feel myself at liberty to secure the publication of my work
by applying elsewhere.*

I am, Gentlemen, etc., etc.,

M. A. D.

Direct to Mrs. Ashton Dennis,

Post Office, Southampton

April 5, 1809.

What Jane always did, and what you must do, is to write to people in whichever way you think fit. The people she loves are always "My dear" and "My dearest" and she isn't ashamed to express true affection when she feels it, for example, "I love Martha more than ever" in a letter to Cassandra on January 9th, 1799. Some letters are signed "with my love to you all" or "my love to everybody." Sometimes she is "Jane Austen," sometimes "J. A.," and sometimes just plain "Jane."

Her letters to family and friends are filled with gossip and domestic details tailored to suit the recipient. We have to remember that these were private letters, and the more one reads, the more one understands why Cassandra destroyed portions of them. With two brothers away at sea, Jane must have wondered if some letters would arrive, but she kept on writing.

Mary Crawford in *Mansfield Park* sums up just how one-sided the relationship can be: "What strange creatures brothers are! You would not write to each other but upon the most urgent necessity in the world; and when obliged to take up the pen to say that such a horse is ill, or such a relation dead, it is done in the fewest possible words. You have but one style among you. I know it perfectly ... very often it is nothing more than—'Dear Mary, I am just arrived. Bath seems full, and everything as usual. Yours sincerely.' That is the true manly style; that is a complete brother's letter." * Fanny Price's sailor brother, William, wrote her long letters back—not all men are Henry Crawfords. Take your cue from how Jane moderates her style to fit the purpose of the letter and its recipient. Among the letters that Cassandra kept from Jane was a copy of the letter from Mrs. Ashton Dennis of Southampton to the publishers Crosby and Co.

These publishers had bought, some six years previously, a novel entitled "Susan." They had undertaken to publish it; it was the author's first work. Imagine the thrill of knowing that your first novel is going to be published, and then the

* *MP*, Ch6

disappointment, embarrassment, and frustration when the publishers sit on it for six years. We know that the manuscript was *Northanger Abbey*, and the furious author was Jane. The Mr. Seymour in the letter was a business associate of her brother, Henry, who was acting as her agent. Jane wanted to remain anonymous (a lady would not have a public profile as an author), but perhaps, even more, she wanted to tell them (in a polite and business-like way) that they had better publish her novel or return it. She wasn't just cross—by using the pseudonym Mrs. Ashton Dennis, she could tell them that she was M.A.D.

Your e-mails, letters, and texts will say so much more if you suit the style to the purpose and the recipient. Stick to your guns. You can be like Jane, remaining polite and still signing off in the way you want to. Jane wouldn't bestow her kisses on just anybody and neither should you.

SHOULD I CHOOSE LIFE EXPERIENCE OR WORK EXPERIENCE?

Q YOU HAVE THE OPTION OF GOING TO COLLEGE, BUT YOU'RE NOT SURE IF YOU'RE READY FOR IT RIGHT NOW—OR IF YOU'LL EVER BE READY. IN FACT, YOU THINK IT MIGHT BE BEST TO SKIP THE ALLEGED "BEST YEARS OF YOUR LIFE" ALTOGETHER AND GO STRAIGHT INTO BUILDING A CAREER. SHOULD YOU HEAD OFF TO COLLEGE AND MAYBE SEE SOME OF THE WORLD IN THE LONG SUMMER VACATIONS, OR PLAY IT SAFE AND SETTLE DOWN IN A SENSIBLE JOB?

> *Mr. Allen, who owned the chief of the property about Fullerton, the village in Wiltshire where the Morlands lived, was ordered to Bath for the benefit of a gouty constitution—and his lady, a good-humored woman, fond of Miss Morland, and probably aware that if adventures will not befall a young lady in her own village, she must seek them abroad, invited her to go with them.*
>
> NORTHANGER ABBEY

A The most important thing for you to do is Something. Adventures will not befall you if you stay at home. Perhaps college is not for you, but you will probably regret it if you throw yourself into the rat race without first seeing what the alternatives are.

Jane Austen didn't have the chance to go to college—it wasn't a possibility for girls (or most boys!) in the late 1700s. I think that she'd have loved to go. She must have envied her student brothers' lives at Oxford. Francis and Charles, the two youngest boys, were sent to the Naval Academy in Portsmouth instead of to university; Edward got to take a "Grand Tour," visiting other European countries. Most of the Austen brothers visited places Jane could only dream of. I think there are echoes of this longing in Catherine Morland who, like Jane, at least gets to visit Bath:

"... They determined on walking round Beechen Cliff, that noble hill whose beautiful verdure and hanging coppice render it so striking an object from almost every opening in Bath.

'I never look at it,' said Catherine, as they walked along the side of the river, 'without thinking of the south of France.'

'You have been abroad then?' said Henry, a little surprised.

'Oh! No, I only mean what I have read about. It always puts me in mind of the country that Emily and her father traveled through, in The Mysteries of Udolpho.'" *

Jane would warn you against throwing away opportunities. You don't want to end up exclaiming, like Laura in Love and Freindship [sic]: "'Alas! What probability is there of my ever tasting the Dissipations of London, the Luxuries of Bath or the stinking Fish of Southampton?'" Jane often sent her heroines off on travels. Their trips are minor by our standards, but before they could choose to settle down, their worlds opened up. Jane never left Britain, but she still traveled to make visits and work with her publisher. Her work might have been poorer without it.

Don't turn your nose up at possibilities. Your version of Pemberley might be somewhere surprising.

* NA, Ch14

FASHION & STYLE

DETAILS MAY CHANGE BUT THE DILEMMAS
REMAIN THE SAME. WHICH SHOES TO CHOOSE?
IS THIS TOO YOUNG FOR ME? WHAT SHOULD
I WEAR ON MY BIG NIGHT OUT? HOW CAN
I BREAK BAD SHOPPING HABITS? JANE AUSTEN
COULD TRIM A BONNET AND MEND A
PETTICOAT WITH THE BEST OF THEM,
AND HER NOVELS AND LETTERS SHOW
A KEEN EYE FOR THE TELLING DETAIL.
LET JANE BE YOUR STYLE GURU.

HEELS OR FLATS?

Q CHOOSING THE RIGHT SHOES HAS BEEN A DILEMMA FOR CENTURIES. WHEN IT COMES TO FOOTWEAR, YOU PRETTY MUCH STICK TO FLAT SHOES IN CASE "FALLING HEAD OVER HEELS" BECOMES MORE REALITY THAN METAPHOR. BUT YOU CAN'T HELP ENVYING YOUR BALANCE-GIFTED FRIENDS WHO STEP OUT IN STUNNING FOUR-INCHERS, TURNING HEADS LIKE THEY'RE ON THE RED CARPET. IS IT WORTH RISKING YOUR SAFETY FOR THE GLAMOR OF HEELS?

I am afraid I cannot undertake to carry Martha's shoes home, for, though we had plenty of room in our trunks when we came, we shall have many more things to take back, and I must allow besides for my packing.

LETTER TO CASSANDRA, BATH, JUNE 2ND, 1799

A This has been a dilemma for centuries and would have been a question for Jane Austen and her heroines to ask themselves. Jane loved shopping and was reluctant to make room in her luggage for purchases for anybody else. She did agree to carry the shoes home for Martha, but she wasn't willing to give up too much space. "At any rate," she said in the same letter "they shall all have flat heels." Flat shoes took up less space, but they weren't a frumpy option.

Jane's was a time of gorgeous shoes, the kind that people would covet today—handmade, the softest leather or prettiest silk, beautiful colors, and decorated with buckles, ribbons, embroidery, flowers, and all manner of cute things. There were many styles to choose from; court shoes had a heel and were more substantial than the delightful little shoes worn for dancing. Both men and women were thrilled by the latest fashions. In *Sanditon*, Mr. P., a founder of a new seaside town, muses over the implications of a window display: "'Civilization, Civilization indeed!' cried Mr. P., delighted—'Look my dear Mary—Look at William Heeley's windows.— Blue Shoes, and nankin Boots!—Who would have expected such a sight at a Shoemaker's in old Sanditon!—This is new within the Month. There was no blue Shoe when we passed this way a month ago.—Glorious indeed!'" *

If you visit Jane Austen's House Museum in Chawton, you'll be able to see a pair of exquisite ivory silk slippers that belonged to her niece, Marianne Knight. They are just the kind of thing a girl nowadays might want, but we'd call them "ballet flats." You'll also be able to walk the short distance along the Gosport Road to the far grander Chawton House once owned by Jane's brother, Edward. It's easy to imagine how muddy and dank the road might have been in Jane's time, although it might be better not to— conditions could be pretty disgusting. When in city or country, good boots were another absolute essential.

* S, Ch4

Lord Osborne makes awkward
conversation with Emma Watson:
"Have you been walking this morning?"
"No, my lord; we thought it too dirty."
"You should wear half-boots." After another pause: *"Nothing sets off a neat
ankle more than a half-boot; nankeen galoshed with black looks very well.
Do not you like half-boots?"*

THE WATSONS

When Elizabeth Bennet set out to walk from Longbourn to Netherfield, she was probably wearing a pair of boots that laced someway up the calf. They couldn't have stopped her petticoats from getting muddy, but they would have helped to keep her feet dry.

Both Jane and Cassandra also often wore wooden pattens to protect their shoes and lift themselves several inches above the filthy or muddy streets. This was recalled decades later in the memoir that their nephew, James Edward Austen-Leigh, wrote along with his two sisters: "When the roads were dirty, the sisters took long walks in pattens. This defence against wet and dirt is now seldom seen. The few that remain are banished from good society, and employed only in menial work." *

The Victorians might have banished pattens, but who would want to be uncomfortable in impractical footwear or ruin a pair of beautiful and expensive shoes? Pattens and boots were sensible and just as useful as boots today. Jane and Cassandra knew that they had to be suitably shod for every occasion.

*Austen-Leigh, J. E., ed. Sutherland, K. (2008)

Snow causes consternation at a Christmas Eve party in *Emma* when Mr. John Knightley delivers the news that the ground is covered and heavy snow is still falling. The heroine's sister, Isabella, is desperate to get home to her children, but is wearing the wrong shoes:

"'You had better order the carriage directly, my love,' said she; 'I dare say we shall be able to get along, if we set off directly; and if we do come to any thing very bad, I can get out and walk. I am not at all afraid. I should not mind walking half the way. I could change my shoes, you know, the moment I got home; and it is not the sort of thing that gives me cold.'

'Indeed!' replied he [her husband]. 'Then, my dear Isabella, it is the most extraordinary sort of thing in the world, for in general every thing does give you cold. Walk home!—you are prettily shod for walking home, I dare say. It will be bad enough for the horses.'" *

Isabella has arrived by carriage and is wearing party shoes—her flats, the equivalent of our impractical heels. It turns out that the snow isn't that deep, and Isabella and her pretty slippers get home safely.

Flats were the fashion essential, but Isabella could have had a more practical alternative with her—boots or even pattens. She could have worn or brought something sturdier with her, and carried her glamorous shoes home in a sweet little bag. So—heels or flats? The answer is both, and you need some boots as well.

* *E*, Ch15

WHAT CAN I DO TO CONTROL MY SHOPPING BINGES?

WE ALL NEED A LITTLE PICK-ME-UP OCCASIONALLY, AND THAT BOOST OFTEN TAKES THE FORM OF VERY PRETTY THINGS. ABOUT ONCE A YEAR, YOU GET TIRED OF WINDOW SHOPPING AND BUY ALL THE ITEMS YOU HAD PREVIOUSLY DENIED YOURSELF. YOU CAN PRETTY MUCH AFFORD IT—THE SHOPPING SPREES DON'T PUT YOU IN THE POORHOUSE, ALTHOUGH YOU DO CARRY A CREDIT CARD BALANCE FOR A FEW MONTHS AFTER—BUT YOU ALWAYS FEEL GUILTY FOR SPENDING THE MONEY. CAN YOU DO ANYTHING TO ALLEVIATE THE EMOTIONAL FALLOUT OR DO YOU HAVE TO GIVE UP THE SHOPPING SPREE?

Everybody likes to go a little crazy sometimes and if you can pretty much afford it, is there a problem? Most people get bored, and perhaps if you didn't leave it a whole year between these sprees, you might get more enjoyment and less guilt from them. *The Beautifull Cassandra*, written by Jane when she was a girl, captures the longing for something different perfectly (see pages 146–147). Everybody needs to escape from the mundane.

Instead of suddenly falling in love with an elegant bonnet and needing to eat six ices without paying, you should probably plan for a more controlled spree each season. Think about what you actually want (and, more importantly, need) and then go shopping. You'll have just as much fun and a lot less guilt. This is what Jane did. In Georgian times, shopping was already a much-loved activity. A Hampshire girl like Jane had to content herself with the local shops, while carefully planning trips farther afield to larger, fashionable places like London, Southampton, and Bath. She and Cassandra would go armed with lists of what they both wanted and needed, and spend a lot of time looking for exactly the right pattern or fabric or trimming for a hat. Jane rattles on to Cassandra in this letter written at Christmas 1798: "... I am full of joy at much of your information; that you should have been to a ball, and have danced at it, and supped with the Prince, and that you should meditate the purchase of a new muslin gown, are delightful circumstances. *I* am determined to buy a handsome one whenever I can, and I am so tired and ashamed of half my present stock, that I even blush at the sight of the wardrobe which contains them ..."

"I cannot determine what to do about my new gown; I wish such things were to be bought ready-made ..."

"I insist upon your persevering in your intention of buying a new gown; I am sure you must want one, and as you will have 5l. due in a week's time, I am certain you may afford it very well ..."

"Of my charities to the poor since I came home you shall have a faithful account. I have given a pair of worsted stockings to Mary Hutchins, Dame Kew, Mary Steevens, and Dame Staples; a shift to Hannah Staples, and a shawl to Betty Dawkins; amounting in all to about half a guinea ..." *

Pay attention—here's the other way to avoid feeling guilty about shopping trips—give away things you don't want or need any more!

* Letter to Cassandra, Steventon, December 24th, 1798

145

The Beautifull Cassandra
by Jane Austen

dedicated by permission to Miss Austen.

Dedication.
Madam

You are a Phoenix. Your taste is refined, your Sentiments are noble,
and your Virtues innumerable. Your Person is lovely, your Figure, elegant,
and your Form, magestic. Your Manners are polished, your Conversation
is rational and your appearance singular. If therefore the following Tale
will afford one moment's amusement to you, every wish will be gratified of
Your most obedient
humble servant
The Author

Chapter the First
Cassandra was the Daughter and the only Daughter of a celebrated
Millener in Bond Street. Her father was of noble Birth, being the near
relation of the Dutchess of _____'s Butler.

Chapter the 2d
When Cassandra had attained her 16th year, she was lovely and amiable
and chancing to fall in love with an elegant Bonnet, her Mother had just
compleated bespoke by the Countess of _____ she placed it on her gentle
Head and walked from her Mother's shop to make her Fortune.

Chapter the 3d
The first person she met, was the Viscount of _____ a young Man, no less
celebrated for his Accomplishments and Virtues, than for his Elegance and
Beauty. She curtseyed and walked on.

Chapter the 4th
She then proceeded to a Pastry-cooks where she devoured six ices, refused to
pay for them, knocked down the Pastry Cook and walked away.

Chapter the 5th
She next ascended a Hackney Coach and ordered it to Hampstead, where she was no sooner arrived than she ordered the Coachman to turn round and drive her back again.

Chapter the 6th
Being returned to the same spot of the same Street she had sate out from, the Coachman demanded his Pay.

Chapter the 7th
She searched her pockets over again and again; but every search was unsuccessfull. No money could she find. The man grew peremptory. She placed her bonnet on his head and ran away.

Chapter the 8th
Thro' many a street she then proceeded and met in none the least Adventure till on turning a Corner of Bloomsbury Square, she met Maria.

Chapter the 9th
Cassandra started and Maria seemed surprised; they trembled, blushed, turned pale and passed each other in a mutual silence.

Chapter the 10th
Cassandra was next accosted by her freind the Widow, who squeezing out her little Head thro' her less window, asked her how she did? Cassandra curtseyed and went on.

Chapter the 11th
A quarter of a mile brought her to her paternal roof in Bond Street from which she had now been absent nearly 7 hours.

Chapter the 12th
She entered it and was pressed to her Mother's bosom by that worthy Woman. Cassandra smiled and whispered to herself "This is a day well spent."

Finis

HOW DO I REFORM AN OVERZEALOUS FOLLOWER OF FASHION?

Q YOUR FRIEND SEEMS TO HAVE LITTLE SENSE AND A LOT OF MONEY WHEN IT COMES TO FASHION. SHE'LL BUY ALMOST ANYTHING SHE SEES IN THE LATEST MAGAZINE, WHETHER OR NOT IT LOOKS GOOD ON HER (OR ANYONE ELSE FOR THAT MATTER). AS SUCH, SHE OFTEN WEARS UNFLATTERING CLOTHES THAT MAKE HER LOOK MUCH LESS ATTRACTIVE THAN SHE REALLY IS. AND, OF COURSE, THE AMOUNT OF MONEY SHE SPENDS ON ONE-USE CLOTHING IS BECOMING AN ISSUE. CAN YOU STEER HER IN A MORE SENSIBLE (AND FLATTERING) DIRECTION WITHOUT BEING TOO INSULTING ABOUT HER APPEARANCE?

A It's kind of you to be so concerned about your friend, but you'll have to remember that you are not her mother, and what she does with her money is really up to her. Gently trying to steer her is all you can do. When Jane Austen's characters make fashion or shopping mistakes, it is because she wants to show us something lacking in them. In real life, Jane knew that even the most delightful of nieces could take an annoyingly long time dithering in a shop or buy something in a hurry and regret it. You must first of all try to discern what kind of a foolish shopper your friend is.

Emma Woodhouse's friend, Harriet Smith, could have done with advice on shopping instead of on her love life: "Harriet, tempted by every thing and swayed by half a word, was always very long at a purchase; and while she was still hanging over muslins and changing her mind, Emma went to the door for amusement." *

* E, Ch27

Lydia Bennet makes
an impulse buy:

*"Look here, I have bought this
bonnet. I do not think it is very
pretty; but I thought I might as
well buy it as not …" And when
her sisters abused it as ugly, she
added, with perfect unconcern,
"Oh! but there were two or three
much uglier in the shop …"*

PRIDE AND PREJUDICE

Emma finds it more fun to watch the world go by and chat to Frank Churchill than pay attention to what Harriet is doing. But eventually she joins Harriet "at the interesting counter, trying, with all the force of her own mind, to convince her that if she wanted plain muslin it was of no use to look at figured; and that a blue ribbon, be it ever so beautiful, would still never match her yellow pattern." *

All Harriet needed was a little guidance. Remember that she was almost alone in the world. If your friend is a Harriet Smith, stick by her and try to make tactful suggestions, but don't start matchmaking.

If your friend is like Robert Ferrars in *Sense and Sensibility*, you might as well give up; what he buys and even the way that he goes about buying it tell us right away that he is somebody to be avoided. Bad shopping habits are not the sole preserve of women.

* E, Ch27

Elinor and Marianne Dashwood are on the sad business of selling some of their mother's jewelry. Robert Ferrars doesn't know this, but he rudely keeps them and everybody else waiting: "He was giving orders for a toothpick-case for himself, and till its size, shape, and ornaments were determined,—all of which, after examining and debating for a quarter of an hour over every toothpick-case in the shop, were finally arranged by his own inventive fancy,—he had no leisure to bestow any other attention on the two ladies, than what was comprised in three or four very broad stares ..." Elinor notices (and she's not very impressed) that he is "adorned in the first style of fashion." *

If your friend is like Robert, don't waste anymore time. Leave him to his bejeweled indulgences.

Isabella Thorpe in *Northanger Abbey* is just as bad. She was influenced by all the wrong things—what was in fashion, instead of what suited her, and what she thought particular men might like: "'I wear nothing but purple now: I know I look hideous in it, but no matter — it is your dear brother's favorite color.'" †

* *S&S*, Ch33. † *NA*, Ch27

150

If your friend is as shallow and nasty as Isabella, Jane would advise you to run a mile and to look for somebody like Eleanor Tilney, who understood what was elegant, and what suited her, and was a much better friend to Catherine.

If your friend is worth bothering with, but is just a little misguided when it comes to clothes, try offering advice that is very specific or buying her little presents of things that you think will suit her. Jane, Cassandra, and their closest friends all helped each other when it came to buying clothes, shoes, and hats. They offered advice about what looked nicest.

In Jane's time, just as today, illustrations of the latest fashions appeared in magazines. We can imagine them planning their purchases before they went shopping together or on each other's behalf. You could try this, too. They discussed how much things cost and the best places to buy things. Tell your friend what you think and listen to her advice as well (even if you ignore it completely). Jane often mentions wearing things that have been given or lent to her; offer to lend your friend things for particular occasions as well, accessories or actual garments.

Here's Jane writing to her sister in a mock serious tone. She wants to be sure that Cassandra will be seen to the best advantage. White was the only color to wear. Not to wear it would be like turning up in something whacky or frumpy when everybody else was in a little black shift dress.

As you have by this time received my last letter, it is fit that I should begin another, and I begin with the hope, which is at present uppermost in my mind, that you often wore a white gown in the morning at the time of all the gay parties being with you ...

LETTER TO CASSANDRA, STEVENTON, JANUARY 3RD, 1801

WHAT SHOULD I WEAR TO AN INTERVIEW?

YOU WORK IN A JOB THAT'S PRETTY CASUAL ABOUT CLOTHES; JEANS AND T-SHIRTS ARE AN ACCEPTED UNIFORM IN YOUR OFFICE EVERY DAY OF THE WEEK. HOWEVER, YOU'VE GOT A BIG INTERVIEW COMING UP AT A NEW COMPANY, AND YOU'RE NOT SURE WHAT THEIR DRESS CODE IS. ON THE ONE HAND, YOU DON'T WANT TO FEEL OVERDRESSED IF

YOUR INTERVIEWER IS WEARING FLIP-FLOPS. ON THE OTHER, WHAT IF YOU LOOK LIKE A GRUNGY HIPPIE WHILE THEY'RE IN A BUTTONED-UP SUIT? HOW CAN YOU MAKE SURE YOU'RE SAFE WHATEVER THE SCENARIO?

You must imagine that you will face the interview panel from hell— Caroline Bingley and Louisa Hurst. In everyday life, those two are not who you should be trying to please, but when it comes to things like job interviews, you should prepare to have your worst fears realized. You need to show them what an excellent employee you will be and that you will act appropriately in any setting. This isn't about hurrying across the fields because you are worried about your sister, or strolling in looking as though you've been to the beach. Choose clothes and shoes that are neat and tidy by a modern-day Caroline Bingley's standards. Don't give her any grounds to start abusing you the moment you are out of the room.

In Jane's letters, we can sometimes detect slight impatience with the time-consuming business of dress and ornamentation. Perhaps she sometimes goes into detail because she knows that Cassandra will want it, or just because the correspondence is about choosing things.

"I am not to wear my white satin cap to-night, after all; I am to wear a mamalouc cap instead, which Charles Fowle sent to Mary, and which she lends me. It is all the fashion now; worn at the opera, and by Lady Mildmays at Hackwood balls. I hate describing such things, and I dare say you will be able to guess what it is like ..." *

In another letter (although there is quite possibly some false modesty here) she says: "I wore my aunt's gown ... and my hair was at least tidy, which was all my ambition." †

Perhaps Cassandra had once scolded her for how she dressed; or perhaps the scene with Lizzy's muddy petticoat and blowsy hair, and saying that her only ambition had been to have tidy hair, were because of a critical comment somebody once made.

> *Miss Bingley began abusing her as soon as she was out of the room ... Mrs. Hurst thought the same ...*
>
> *"She has nothing, in short, to recommend her, but being an excellent walker. I shall never forget her appearance this morning. She really looked almost wild."*
>
> *"... Her hair, so untidy, so blowsy!"*
>
> *"Yes, and her petticoat; I hope you saw her petticoat, six inches deep in mud, I am absolutely certain; and the gown which had been let down to hide it, not doing its office."*
>
> PRIDE AND PREJUDICE

But writers aren't often known for their tidiness. When they are working, they are likely to be in some approximation of pajamas, living on peanut butter on toast. The public self is altogether different. Jane knew that if she was going to a ball or out visiting, she must do her best to look the part, even if she may not have felt like it. Don't give Caroline Bingley any excuse to shred your résumé. Dress to impress.

* Letter to Cassandra, Steventon, January 8th, 1799. † Letter to Cassandra, Steventon, November 20th, 1800

IS THE DESIGNER LABEL REALLY THAT IMPORTANT?

Q YOU AND YOUR BEST FRIEND HAVE ALWAYS BOUGHT EACH OTHER EXPENSIVE BIRTHDAY PRESENTS, AND WITH HER BIRTHDAY COMING UP, SHE'S BEEN EYEING A PARTICULAR PAIR OF DESIGNER SUNGLASSES AND DROPPING SOME PRETTY HEAVY HINTS. ALTHOUGH YOU WOULDN'T USUALLY HESITATE TO BUY THEM FOR HER, YOU'RE JUST A LITTLE LIGHT IN THE WALLET AT THE MOMENT. LUCKILY, YOU'VE SEEN A VERY GOOD KNOCKOFF DESIGN AT A MUCH MORE REASONABLE PRICE. IF YOU GIVE HER THE KNOCKOFF PAIR, WILL SHE NOTICE? MORE TO THE POINT, IS IT WORTH THE RISK THAT SHE WILL?

A I'm afraid that your best friend will definitely notice. She will think that you missed the point completely or don't want to bother. You need to take some shopping tips from Jane Austen.

Jane and Cassandra often shopped for each other and undertook commissions for family and friends. Letters flew back and forth while they decided exactly what to buy. The sisters had to be very careful with their money, so although they liked lovely things, they had to weigh up the pros and cons of every purchase. It is clear that quality is what mattered: "I like the stockings also very much, and greatly prefer having two pair only of that quality to three of an inferior sort." * Jane thanked her sister, who had quite a list of commissions to perform.

If your best friend is being precise about the sunglasses she wants, it is because it matters to her. She will notice the quality difference, even if they look exactly the same to you. She is just like Jane and Cassandra in that she won't want inferior versions.

* Letter to Cassandra, Steventon, October 26th, 1800

Sometimes we think we have a bargain in our sights, only to find out that there's a good reason why the price is so low. Jane goes through just this when she's shopping: "Now I will give you the history of Mary's veil ... I had no difficulty in getting a muslin veil for half a guinea, and not much more in discovering afterwards that the muslin was thick, dirty, and ragged, and therefore would by no means do for a united gift. I changed it consequently as soon as I could ... I thought myself lucky in getting a black lace one for sixteen shillings. I hope the half of that sum will not greatly exceed what you had intended to offer upon the altar of sister-in-law affection." *

If you cannot afford the sunglasses all by yourself, I'm afraid you may just have to come out and say it; be as candid about money as Jane and Cassandra were. Or perhaps you should do what they were doing for their sister-in-law—find somebody to join forces with you and make "a united gift."

My cloak came on Tuesday, and, though I expected a good deal, the beauty of the lace astonished me. It is too handsome to be worn— almost too handsome to be looked at ... We find no fault with your manner of performing any of our commissions ...

LETTER TO CASSANDRA, STEVENTON, NOVEMBER 1ST 1800

* Letter to Cassandra, Bath, June 9th, 1799

SHOULD I DRESS TO LOOK GREAT OR LOOK MY AGE?

 YOU'RE LONG OUT OF YOUR TWENTIES, AND YOUR THIRTIES ARE JUST ABOUT TO BECOME A MEMORY, BUT YOU STILL HAVE A YOUTHFUL FIGURE THAT YOU LIKE TO SHOW OFF. YOU DON'T WEAR ANYTHING TOO INAPPROPRIATE, BUT YOU DO TEND TO FAVOR A SHORTER SKIRT. YOU FEEL THAT WHILE YOU HAVE IT, YOU MIGHT AS WELL FLAUNT IT. HOWEVER, YOU WORRY THAT YOU MIGHT BE GIVING THE WRONG IMPRESSION OR, EVEN WORSE, DRESSING MUTTON AS LAMB. SHOULD YOU SUCCUMB TO THE FASHION CONSTRAINTS OF MIDDLE AGE OR CONTINUE TO DRESS IN A MORE FLATTERING MANNER?

It was the same room in which we danced fifteen years ago. I thought it all over, and in spite of the shame of being so much older, felt with thankfulness that I was quite as happy now as then. We paid an additional shilling for our tea, which we took as we chose in an adjoining and very comfortable room.

LETTER TO CASSANDRA, SOUTHAMPTON, DECEMBER 9TH, 1808

 Jane Austen would spot your problem in your phrasing. You don't have to pick between dressing in a flattering way *or* to suit your age— you can do both. Jane was in her thirties when she wrote that she was just as happy as she had been when she was a teenager. She had gone to this ball with her best friend, Martha, and it was a lovely night out. In 1808, one's thirties were more like one's forties today. In the same letter, she tells Cassandra that the only sad thing was seeing so many young girls standing about with too much exposed flesh and nobody to dance with.

Now that you are older and wiser, you're more interested in pleasing yourself than others. Teenagers' nights out often consist of fashion faux-pas and disappointment. You can have a grand night out with your best friend, instead. A thirty-something Jane wouldn't have gone tottering out on a freezing night in heels, a miniskirt, and a skimpy top, but she didn't just sit and watch either— on that night in Southampton she danced with a mysterious gentleman who had nice dark eyes.

Jane had some great times in the years before she died, tragically young. She was earning nice sums from her books and was able to enjoy herself—you should do the same. We know that Jane splurged a little on clothes as her income increased. You, too, can probably afford some lovelier outfits now that you've found your way in the world. You're more confident than you used to be, so why not dress the part?

Had Jane lived, I think we would have seen her heroines getting older. Anne Elliot in *Persuasion* is twenty-seven—significantly older than heroines of earlier works. At the start of the novel, Anne has lost her looks through years of sadness after breaking things off with Captain Wentworth; but as she grows happier and life gets more interesting, she begins to bloom again. Emma Woodhouse's governess finds love "late" in life and becomes Mrs. Weston. Jane kept hoping that her friend, Miss Sharp, another governess, would, too: "She writes highly of Sir Wm. [Sir William Pilkington] I do so want him to marry her. Oh, Sir Wm.! Sir Wm.! how I will love you if you will love Miss Sharp!" *

For Jane, middle age wasn't about giving up; it was about enjoying what one had earned, being free of the anxieties of youth and open to the new possibilities middle age brings. Dress accordingly.

* Letter to Cassandra, Chawton, June 23rd, 1814

WHAT'S THE BEST WAY TO DEAL WITH A COPYCAT?

Q YOU REALLY ENJOY HANGING OUT WITH A FRIEND OF YOURS. SHE'S GOT A GREAT PERSONALITY AND YOU CAN TALK ABOUT NOTHING FOR HOURS. BUT SHE SEEMS TO BE USING YOU AS HER PERSONAL SHOPPER AND RUNS OUT AND BUYS ANOTHER OF WHATEVER YOU BUY. IT'S SO BAD THAT PEOPLE ARE COMMENTING ON THE SIMILARITIES AND CALLING YOU TWINS. YOU DON'T WANT TO HURT HER FEELINGS, BUT YOU'RE FED UP WITH HAVING A CLOTHING CLONE. HOW DO YOU GET HER TO STOP COPYING YOU AND START THINKING FOR HERSELF?

A Jane Austen might ask if you were quite certain of who was dictating whose fashion sense. If people call you twins, are you sure that your friend is copying you? It might be that you are just firm friends, with a lot in common. Have you considered the possibility that you might be her copycat? Jane would urge you to think carefully before you say anything hurtful.

Perhaps it's a simple case of shared fashion sense. The Austen sisters certainly shared one. Their niece Anna paints what I think is a lovely picture of them braving the muddy lanes of Hampshire together. This was very early in the nineteenth century, a while before the spread of

I recollect the frequent visits of my two Aunts, & how they walked in wintry weather through the sloppy lane between Steventon and Dean [sic] in pattens, usually worn at the time even by Gentlewomen. I remember too their bonnets: because though precisely alike in colour, shape & material, I made it a pleasure to guess, & I believe always guessed right, which bonnet & which Aunt belonged to each other.*

RECOLLECTION OF ANNA LEFROY, NÉE AUSTEN, IN AUSTEN-LEIGH, W. & R.A. (1989)

tarred road surfaces. Some biographers think that the sisters' matching bonnets speak of an early descent into middle age, but I think this is just the typical behavior of close sisters (or friends). Jane and Cassandra consulted and helped each other with purchases, and they also shared tastes. I have lost count of the times that my sisters and I have independently bought exactly the same things. Perhaps you are lucky enough to have found a kindred spirit—don't push her away.

Emma Woodhouse really does have a copycat friend. Emma has to learn not to manipulate Harriet Smith, while Harriet has to learn that Miss Woodhouse is not always right. Emma helps Harriet in improving her tastes, manners, and deportment and introduces her to a wider group of people, but she almost costs Harriet her happiness as a result.

At first, having a devoted follower flatters Emma's vanity. Mr. Elton praises Harriet because he wants to worm his way into Emma's heart: "'You have given Miss Smith all that she required,' said he; 'you have made her graceful and easy. She was a beautiful creature when she came to you, but, in my opinion, the attractions you have added are infinitely superior to what she received from nature.'" *

* *E*, Ch6 (1989).

Eventually Emma realizes where she has gone wrong: "Mr. Knightley had spoken prophetically, when he once said, 'Emma, you have been no friend to Harriet Smith.'—She was afraid she had done her nothing but disservice." *

It's very lucky that nice Robert Martin asks Harriet a second time to marry him, and that Harriet has realized where her future happiness lies. This time she doesn't wait to ask Emma what she thinks, she trusts her own judgment and says yes.

After this, her friendship with Emma is much healthier: "Harriet,

> *Kitty, to her very material advantage, spent the chief of her time with her two elder sisters. In society so superior to what she had generally known, her improvement was great. She was not of so ungovernable a temper as Lydia: and, removed from the influence of Lydia's example, she became, by proper attention and management, less irritable, less ignorant, and less insipid.*
>
> PRIDE AND PREJUDICE

necessarily drawn away by her engagements with the Martins, was less and less at Hartfield; which was not to be regretted. The intimacy between her and Emma must sink; their friendship must change into a calmer sort of goodwill; and, fortunately, what ought to be, and must be, seemed already beginning, and in the most gradual, natural manner." †

You don't have to be younger or poorer to be in somebody's shadow. Although Kitty Bennet is older than her sister Lydia, she could easily have followed in her unfortunate footsteps. At first, as the youngest two Bennet girls, they are inseparable. You have to feel a little sorry for Kitty as an insignificant middling one. Jane and Lizzy are distinguished by being the eldest, very close and favored by their father. Mary is close to Kitty in age, but no fun and has probably always been

* E, Ch47. † E, Ch55

dismissive of her. When Kitty and Lydia tell her about what they've been up to she says: "'… such pleasures … would doubtless be congenial with the generality of female minds. But I confess they would have no charms for *me* …'"

It's no wonder that Kitty allies herself with Lydia. It seems desperately unfair when Lydia is invited to go to Brighton with Mrs. Forster: "Wholly inattentive to her sister's feelings, Lydia flew about the house in restless ecstacy, calling for every one's congratulations, and laughing and talking with more violence than ever …"*

However, it turns out that Kitty is escaping by the skin of her teeth. The answer for Kitty is the same as it is for Harriet—they both need space to grow and form their own opinions. Kitty is not allowed to stay with Lydia and Wickham after their disgraceful behavior. Instead, Jane and Lizzy start paying her more attention (about time!) and she flourishes.

If you think your copycat really is a copycat, Jane would prescribe a little more distance and suggest that you point your friend toward other role models.

* *P&P*, Ch41

WHAT SHOULD I WEAR TO A BALL?

Q THE CELEBRATIONS YOU USUALLY ATTEND CONSIST OF NIGHTS OUT IN BARS, SIPPING VODKA AND COKE, BEFORE STUMBLING TO A CLUB IN THE EARLY HOURS. BUT NOW ONE OF YOUR FRIENDS HAS INVITED YOU TO HER WORK'S ANNUAL FUNDRAISING BALL. SHE'S A GOOD FRIEND AND YOU'D LIKE TO MAKE THE EFFORT BUT YOU'VE SIMPLY NO IDEA HOW TO DRESS FOR THE OCCASION: SHORT OR LONG DRESS? HAIR UP OR DOWN? JEWELRY OR TRADITIONAL CORSAGE? HEELS OR FLATS? HOW CAN YOU MAKE SURE YOU LOOK THE PART?

A Jane Austen was the veteran of so many balls that she would completely understand your concerns. Sometimes new things were made or bought, quite often they were borrowed. Jane and Cassandra didn't have enough money to make frivolous purchases. Consider vintage—nobody else will be wearing your dress if it's one that your glamorous godmother wore twenty-something years ago. Whatever you wear, make sure that it is stylish, beautiful, and comfortable—you may be dancing until dawn, and this should dictate your choice of shoes. Just like an Austen heroine, you can choose heels or flats.

> *Our ball was rather more amusing than I expected ... The room was tolerably full, and there were, perhaps, thirty couple of dancers. The melancholy part was, to see so many dozen young women standing by without partners, and each of them with two ugly naked shoulders.*
>
> LETTER TO CASSANDRA, SOUTHAMPTON, DECEMBER 9TH, 1808

You will be immortalized in a thousand Facebook photos and this is where the "ugly bare shoulders" message comes in. Have a look at photos from similar occasions online. The biggest, shortest, or lowest cut dress is generally not the most flattering. Regency dresses with their gorgeous fabrics and shapes would serve better than one of the polyester monstrosities of today.

An Austen heroine would have looked at illustrations in magazines for inspiration. You should do that, too—keeping in mind that for over two hundred years models have not been shaped like real women.

Eleanor Tilney in *Northanger Abbey* should be your style inspiration for the ball. She always looked perfect in the kind of effortless way that is anything but. People noticed that she always wore white—it was the fashionable, high-maintenance color, and suggested riches and leisure. White might not be best (you don't want to look as though you are playing brides!) but you should aim to give the same elegant impression.

Eleanor also took trouble with her hair, wearing white beads in it at the dance where she and Catherine Morland met. It's worth investing time in this, just as it was two hundred years ago. Get somebody to help you practice to get ready. Even Fanny Price is helped by her aunt's maid. Hair up is likely, now as in Jane's time, to look more special. Beware of doing anything too extreme. I suspect that the horrible Isabella Thorpe looked pretty dreadful in her fashionable turban, and you don't want to give the Caroline Bingleys of the world anything to mock you for.

Remember, however, that whatever you wear, the person that you should be pleasing is yourself: "It would be mortifying to the feelings of many ladies, could they be made to understand how little the heart of man is affected by what is costly or new in their attire ... Woman is fine for her own satisfaction alone. No man will admire her the more, no woman will like her the better for it." *

* NA, Ch10

HOW CAN I INJECT A LITTLE LIFE INTO THE STUFFY "BUSINESS ATTIRE" I MUST WEAR TO WORK?

YOU WORK IN A PRETTY HIGH-POWERED CAREER, SO YOU SPEND A LOT OF TIME DRESSING UP FOR BUSINESS LUNCHES AND DINNERS. DESPITE HAVING DONE IT SO MANY TIMES, YOU STILL STRUGGLE WITH YOUR FASHION CHOICES— YOU WANT TO BE COMFORTABLE AND SHOW SOME PERSONALITY, BUT YOU STILL NEED TO LOOK APPROPRIATE FOR THE SETTING. WHAT ARE THE RULES REGARDING DRESSING FOR SUCCESS? DOES "FORMAL" HAVE TO MEAN STUFFY, OR DO YOU HAVE SOME LEEWAY TO EXPRESS YOUR INDIVIDUAL STYLE?

Formal does have to mean formal, just as it did in Regency times. You won't do yourself any favors if you become known as the woman who showed up to the Christmas party in a not-quite-right version of something Lady Gaga would wear. Unfortunately, there are too many Caroline Bingleys and Louisa Hursts in this world, and you'll inevitably run into a few of them in your professional life. They were scathing of Elizabeth Bennet when she arrived having walked across the fields from Longbourn to Netherfield. They said that her behavior showed "a most country-town indifference to decorum" * and were appalled by her mud-soaked petticoat.

The secret to abiding (or appearing to abide) by the conventions is in making careful choices. You needn't live in your business clothes, and there will be times when you can get away with something less formal. Jane Austen would have worn a morning dress first thing; much more comfortable than what one wore to go out in.

P&P, Ch8

*I saw some gauzes in a shop in Bath Street yesterday at only 4d. a yard,
but they were not so good or so pretty as mine. Flowers are very much worn,
and fruit is still more the thing.*
*I cannot decide on the fruit till I hear from you again. Besides, I cannot
help thinking that it is more natural to have flowers grow out of the head
than fruit. What do you think on that subject?*

LETTERS TO CASSANDRA, BATH, SUMMER 1799

Empire-line dresses were also easier to wear than what was in fashion either before or after them, but you must follow the prevailing silhouettes of your day. Avoid anything too tight or too revealing. Choose things that are comfortable and that you can actually go for a brisk walk in—just try not to get your petticoat muddy between meetings.

Spend time choosing fabrics as well as shapes. Jane and Cassandra took great pains when they were deciding which material to buy. Natural is always best, so choose only those that Jane might have chosen—silk, linen, velvet, cotton, or wool. The muslins that they talked of were gorgeous gauzy fabrics, often beautifully embroidered. You might not be able to wear a muslin empire-line gown to your meetings, but you can choose to wear fabrics that will keep you fresh and elegant. Often it's the fabric that makes so called "business wear" so unpleasant.

You should also spend time choosing accessories. This is where you can really be yourself and yet abide by convention and not make yourself ridiculous. A clever choice of jewelry, purse, or scarf will impress your colleagues and make you memorable for all the right reasons. But don't go into meetings with fruit growing out of your head. Avoid wackiness.

HOME & GARDEN

JANE AUSTEN KNEW ALL ABOUT RUNNING A
HOUSE AND GARDEN, FEEDING A LARGE FAMILY,
BALANCING THE BOOKS, AND ENTERTAINING
GUESTS. WHETHER SHE WAS LIVING IN BATH, IN
LONDON WITH HENRY, STAYING AT EDWARD'S
GRAND HOUSE IN KENT, OR IN HER OWN
MODEST HOME IN HAMPSHIRE, SHE
UNDERSTOOD THE BEST WAY TO ACHIEVE
DOMESTIC HAPPINESS. HERE, FIND ADVICE FROM
JANE FOR HOUSEHOLDS OF ANY SIZE, AND LET
A LITTLE CHAWTON TRANQUILLITY INTO
YOUR LIFE …

I'M A WALKING HERBICIDE, AND I'VE KILLED AGAIN. ANY DAMAGE CONTROL ADVICE?

Q YOUR SISTER IS A FABULOUS GARDENER, AND HER LITTLE PATCH OF EARTH IS HER PRIDE AND JOY. SHE LEFT YOU IN CHARGE WHILE SHE WAS AWAY FOR A FEW WEEKS, AND NOW, DUE TO YOUR COMPLETE LACK OF GARDENING SKILLS, MOST OF HER PLANTS ARE EITHER DEAD OR DYING. YOU HAVE TWO MORE WEEKS TO HIDE THE BODIES OR BREAK THE BAD NEWS. DO YOU TELL HER NOW OR WAIT UNTIL SHE RETURNS? AND IS THERE ANYTHING YOU CAN DO TO LIMIT THE DAMAGE IN THE MEANTIME?

A We know that the grounds of the Chawton cottage were larger than they are today, but even so, some descendants of the Austens' trees and plants are still there, and the gardens have been restored with beds of herbs, flowers, and vegetables that the family might have chosen. Cassandra was a fine painter, and the garden would have been a creative outlet for her. Jane was often left in your position, and sent her sister updates on how things were coming along. She would have appreciated just how precious Cassandra's plants and hives of bees were, so take some leaves out of Jane's book.

Your sister knew about your lack of green thumbs before she left you in charge, so she shouldn't be too cross with you. However, it's still best to let her know how things are faring. Tell her about the good things as well as those you are worried about. You will probably find that some casualties have perished from natural causes—just withered and died back because they are meant to. Gardeners know that there are good years and bad years for all plants.

> *I am glad you are so well yourself, and wish everybody else were equally so. I will not say that your mulberry-trees are dead, but I am afraid they are not alive.*
>
> LETTER TO CASSANDRA, CHAWTON, MAY 31ST, 1811

I'd advise you to get a second opinion before your sister returns. See if you can enlist the help of somebody who knows what they are doing—they may be able to reassure you and so help you to shrug off some of the blame, as well as tell you if you are watering too much or too little, where to deadhead and where to leave well alone: "Some of the flower seeds are coming up very well, but your mignonette makes a wretched appearance. Miss Benn has been equally unlucky as to hers. She has seed from four different people, and none of it comes up. Our young piony at the foot of the fir-tree has just blown and looks very handsome, and the whole of the shrubbery border will soon be very gay with pinks and sweet-williams, in addition to the columbines already in bloom.

The syringas, too, are coming out. We are likely to have a great crop of Orleans plumbs, but not many greengages ... I believe I told you differently when I first came home, but I can now judge better than I could then." *

The disappointing non-appearance of the mignonette cannot be Jane's fault if even Miss Benn's has failed to appear, and Cassandra will have half forgotten about it by the time she's finished thinking about the peony. She won't be so bothered about the greengages because she knows about the plums.

However, Jane didn't give her all that bad news at once. She left the sad demise of the mulberry bushes until the next letter.

* Letter to Cassandra, Chawton, May 29th, 1811

WHO GETS TO USE THE EXTRA SPACE
IN OUR HOUSE?

DUE TO A RECENT UPTURN IN YOUR FORTUNES, YOU AND YOUR HUSBAND NO LONGER HAVE TO RENT OUT A ROOM IN YOUR HOUSE TO MAKE ENDS MEET. OF COURSE, THIS NOW MEANS YOU HAVE SPARE SPACE TO TURN INTO ANYTHING YOU WANT. BEING A BIG READER, YOU'D LOVE TO HAVE A LIBRARY, BUT YOUR HUSBAND IS MORE OF AN ENTERTAINMENT JUNKIE AND DESPERATELY WANTS A GAMES ROOM. IS THERE A COMPROMISE OR DO YOU HAVE TO FLIP A COIN?

For Charlotte Lucas, separate rooms were the way she managed to survive. Now, I'm not suggesting that you married a Mr. Collins, but you do need somewhere of your own.

In their last years at the family home in Steventon, Jane and Cassandra Austen managed to construct a place for themselves. Their brothers had all gone out into the world—there must have been spare space at last. They had a "dressing room." This was not a walk-in closet, more somewhere they could spend time alone, and where Cassandra could paint and Jane play the piano and write. They furnished it as best they could with a few purchases and by gathering things from other rooms in the rectory. It would have been a haven for the women from muddy boys. Jane said that she always felt "so much more elegant in it than in the parlour." *

Later, at their cottage in Chawton, Jane and Cassandra shared a room that overlooked the yard. One of them was often away, so there would have been some privacy then, but they chose this arrangement instead of having a room each

* Letter to Cassandra, Steventon, December 1st, 1798

(although there would have been swapping around to accommodate visitors). One can almost picture them whispering by moonlight. Their friend Martha Lloyd came to live with them, too, though her rooms were a slight distance away. So how could anybody write under these conditions?

Jane got up early, and we know that she used the dining room with her table positioned by a window—everybody likes a few distractions. It can seem that a writer's whole house is an extension of her desk and I wonder if Mrs. Austen and Cassandra felt that, but I think they were kind and sensible enough to give Jane a wide berth when she was working.

Fanny Price has a sanctuary: *The aspect was so favorable that even without a fire it was habitable in many an early spring and late autumn morning ... The comfort of it in her hours of leisure was extreme. She could go there after anything unpleasant below, and find immediate consolation in some pursuit, or some train of thought at hand. Her plants, her books ... her writing desk ... were all within her reach; or if indisposed for employment, if nothing but musing would do, she could scarcely see an object in that room which had not an interesting remembrance connected with it ... The room was most dear to her, and she would not have changed its furniture for the handsomest in the house ...*

MANSFIELD PARK

You and your husband both need space, whatever your endeavors—be they work or relaxation. If you let him have this room for games, he must let you have a space elsewhere that is particularly yours. Don't try to compromise and share. A nice garage might suit him, or else you could divide the room. Perhaps you could take over the dining room, if you have one, or make a corner of another room particularly yours or his. You must make sure that nobody interferes with your space; for this reason, it might be better to have a corner of a room that nobody will touch instead of a share of a games room where other people will lounge about and be annoying.

> *Elizabeth at first had rather wondered that Charlotte should not prefer the dining parlor for common use; it was a better sized room, and had a pleasanter aspect; but she soon saw that her friend had an excellent reason for what she did, for Mr. Collins would undoubtedly have been much less in his own apartment had they sat in one equally lively; and she gave Charlotte credit for the arrangement.*
>
> PRIDE AND PREJUDICE

Once you have your space, you must make sure that everybody respects it (and does the same for your husband's). If they don't, you will feel like Mr. Bennet when Mr. Collins imposes on his precious library: "Lydia's intention of walking to Meryton was not forgotten; every sister except Mary agreed to go with her; and Mr. Collins was to attend them, at the request of Mr. Bennet, who was most anxious to get rid of him, and have his library to himself; for thither Mr. Collins had followed him after breakfast, and there he would continue, nominally engaged with one of the largest folios in the collection, but really talking to Mr. Bennet, with little cessation, of his house and garden at Hunsford. Such doings discomposed Mr. Bennet exceedingly. In his library he had been always sure of leisure and tranquillity; and though prepared, as he told Elizabeth, to meet with folly and conceit in every other room in the house, he was used to be free from them there; his civility, therefore, was most prompt in inviting Mr. Collins to join his daughters in their walk; and Mr. Collins, being in fact much better fitted for a walker than a reader, was extremely well pleased to close his large book, and go." *

It was in the days just before they moved to Chawton, where the most productive and successful years of Jane's life were to be spent, that she wrote to the publishers who had sat on *Susan* (later *Northanger Abbey*) for years and enquired about getting the manuscript back. It seems that she was anticipating having space and tranquillity at last and being able to focus on her writing. It doesn't much matter which room your space is in, as long as it is yours.

* *P&P*, Ch15

IS IT POSSIBLE TO RECONCILE MY BIG-CITY SENSIBILITY WITH SMALL-TOWN LIVING?

 YOU USED TO LIVE IN A BIG CITY, AND ONE THING YOU APPRECIATED WAS THE ANONYMITY: NO ONE KNEW YOUR BUSINESS UNLESS YOU TOLD THEM. BUT NOW THAT YOU'VE FORSAKEN THE BRIGHT LIGHTS FOR A SMALL COUNTRY TOWN, EVERYONE SEEMS TO KNOW ALL ABOUT YOU. FRANKLY, IT MAKES YOU UNCOMFORTABLE. WILL YOU EVER BE ABLE TO FIND A WAY TO FEEL AT HOME HERE?

 There's an axiom that all great literature is one of two stories; a man goes on a journey or a stranger comes to town. This holds true for Jane Austen's novels, and your life is imitating art at the moment. Try to understand that you are currently just as interesting as Mr. Bingley or Frank Churchill, or Henry or Mary Crawford. It is going to take a while for you to adjust to small-town ways.

You must feel like poor Marianne Dashwood: "Little had Mrs. Dashwood or her daughters imagined, when they first came into Devonshire, that so many engagements would arise to occupy their time as shortly presented themselves, or that they should have such frequent invitations and such constant visitors." *

Marianne doesn't mind this when Willoughby is there, but once he leaves, it's a different matter. She really does feel that she is there to make sport (or at the very least entertainment) for her neighbors, saying: "'The rent of this cottage is said to be low; but we have it on very hard terms, if we are to dine at the park whenever any one is staying either with them or with us.'" †

I'm not suggesting that you take up with a heartbreaker like Willoughby, but perhaps if you had somebody else to hang out with, you wouldn't find life in the sticks so bad. Cultivate some local friends; there must be some kindred spirits.

> Mr. Bennet speaks to Elizabeth:
> "But, Lizzy, you look as if you did not enjoy it. You are not going to be missish, I hope, and pretend to be affronted at an idle report. For what do we live, but to make sport for our neighbors, and laugh at them in our turn?"
> PRIDE AND PREJUDICE

Some people, like Mr. Bingley and Frank Churchill, throw themselves into the life of their new home. You could even be like the Crawfords and get involved in amateur theatricals—it need not end in tears. If you join in with those things that interest you, you might have more fun, but it's not compulsory—you wouldn't catch Jane Fairfax or Mr. Darcy joining the local amateur drama club.

* *S&S*, Ch11. † *S&S*, Ch19

Some people just aren't suited to small-town or country living. Mary Crawford eventually goes back to London, but not without many regrets and a sense that things might have turned out differently if she had chosen to marry the future clergyman she fell for. However, she really missed the shops and being able to do and buy whatever she wanted whenever she wanted. Life as a vicar's wife would not have suited her. The cracks are there, right from the start.

There is the saga of getting her harp transported—she's surprised to find that she cannot find a local willing to do her bidding, however much money she waves about: "'I was astonished to find what a piece of work was made of it! To want a horse and cart in the country seemed impossible, so I told my maid to speak for one directly; and as I cannot look out of my dressing closet without seeing one farmyard, nor walk in the shrubbery without passing another, I thought it would be only ask and have, and was rather grieved that I could not give the advantage to all. Guess my surprise, when I found that I had been asking the most unreasonable, most impossible thing in the world; had offended all the farmers, all the laborers, all the hay in the parish!'" *

Edmund Bertram puts Mary right about the horse and cart; it's harvest-time, and one really can't be spared. Perhaps, like Mary, you are accidentally offending people or stepping on toes, and that's why you have caused such a splash. Is there a kind soul who could let you know that actually, the doctor always parks there, or that the jogger you nearly killed as you screeched past the church is the mailman, or that woman you beat to the last copy of the *People* magazine was the school principal? Try to make a little more time for pleasantries.

Jane loved visiting cities and enjoyed what was offered there, but she found contentment and all she needed to be creative in the countryside, with the small town of Alton a brisk walk away. Here she is writing to her niece, Anna, an aspiring novelist: "You are now collecting your people delightfully, getting them exactly into such a spot as is the delight of my life. Three or four families in a country village is the very thing to work on ..." †

You can be like Mary and retreat, or become like Jane and try to enjoy it all. Perhaps Mr. Bingley should be your model here—he tries to be happy wherever he finds himself.

> "When I am in the country," he [Bingley] replied, "I never wish to leave it; and when I am in town, it is pretty much the same. They have each their advantages, and I can be equally happy in either."
>
> PRIDE AND PREJUDICE

* *MP*, Ch22. † Letter to Anna Austen, Chawton, September 9th, 1814

CAN A LARGE FAMILY FIT INTO A SMALL HOUSE?

Q YOU JUST LOVE CHILDREN AND WANT TO HAVE MORE, BUT YOU'RE QUICKLY RUNNING OUT OF SPACE IN WHICH TO HOUSE THEM. ALTHOUGH YOU DON'T HAVE THE MONEY FOR A BIGGER PLACE, YOU DON'T WANT TO GIVE UP YOUR DREAM OF A LARGE FAMILY TO LOVE AND CARE FOR. CAN YOU MAKE THIS WORK WITH LIMITED SPACE?

> *A family of ten children will be always called a fine family, where there are heads and arms and legs enough for the number ... Mrs. Morland was a very good woman, and wished to see her children everything they ought to be; but her time was so much occupied in lying-in and teaching the little ones, that her elder daughters were inevitably left to shift for themselves ...*
>
> NORTHANGER ABBEY

 Although in later life Jane Austen sometimes expressed weariness and disdain for the constant child-bearing of her sisters-in-law and neighbors, she knew all about the joy of big families. She was one of eight children, and her parents took in extras as pupils. Being an Austen was fun. The rectory might have been full and drafty but there were games, jokes, sports, books, and interesting visitors—and they put on plays right there in the barn. It's a pity that you don't have a big, old vicarage in Hampshire, but even if you did you would still need to make sure everyone was happy. One person's bustle is another person's chaos.

Jane and Cassandra would tell you that you can make it work. Their letters give copious details of family arrangements—the Austen family just kept growing—and the sisters were often wondering and asking how they were going to fit everybody in. But with ingenuity, they did it. This was one of the main concerns about their Chawton home—would it be big enough for the inevitable streams of visitors?

"There are six bedchambers at Chawton; Henry wrote to my mother the other day, and luckily mentioned the number, which is just what we wanted to be assured of. He speaks also of garrets for store places ..." *

It was ever thus—how many bedrooms and how much storage space?

You can imagine the work, the laundry, the planning of meals—it wasn't as though they could just order takeout—supplies had to be husbanded, and sometimes rationed until the next year's harvest. Would the honey last? What about the apples? Here is Jane voicing some of their usual anxieties about

* Letter to Cassandra, Southampton, November 21st, 1808

it all: "... and Mr. and Mrs. Moore and one child are to come on Monday for ten days. I hope Charles and Fanny may not fix the same time, but if they come at all in October they *must*. What is the use of hoping? The two parties of children is the chief evil ..." * Even with Edward's grand houses the arrangements were complex and involved much planning and shuffling.

But they did manage to fit everybody in, and so will you. It's all about attitude. When Louisa Musgrove has her fateful fall from the Cobb in Lyme, she is taken to the Harvilles' small house nearby. Louisa's unexpected stay might flummox

some families, but although their house is already full, the kind Harvilles manage to accommodate her and she is nursed back to health. People are always welcome at the Harvilles' house and they try to make space for everybody, even suggesting hammocks—they were a navy family, after all.

At the opposite end of the spectrum are the Prices. They have a lot of children and limited space, but staying with them is nothing like staying with the Harvilles. The Prices' house was: "the scene of mismanagement and discomfort from beginning to end ... Whatever was wanted was hallooed for, and the servants hallooed out their excuses from the kitchen. The doors were in constant banging, the stairs were never at rest, nothing was done without a clatter, nobody sat still, and nobody could command attention when they spoke." †

* Letter to Cassandra, Godmersham, October 14th, 1813. † *MP*, Ch 39

The Prices' house wasn't tiny so it didn't have to be that way. I think that Jane would advise you to go ahead and have a big family if you want to, but make sure that you'll be like the Harvilles and not the Prices. Can your full little home be harmonious and happy? Would you be able to cheerfully accommodate Louisa Musgrove if she happens to fall off a wall nearby?

The other thing to keep in mind is the impact on children of being so many. It's almost all positive, but like Catherine Morland, your older children will often have to "shift for themselves"; but being able to look after oneself and help out with the younger children is no bad thing.

If you want the big family, you'll have to be creative, economical, and to put up with a lot of mud. One of the secrets of the Austens' happy family life must have been that they lived in the country. Catherine Morland loved cricket, baseball, and riding around the countryside, and the Austens did, too. I think that Jane would say that access to outdoor space is an essential—although hunting certainly isn't.

If your kids are going to end up like Edward and Francis "Fly" Austen, you'll need to have a place to escape to. We know that the Austen girls loved having a bit more space when their brothers had all left home. Jane's comment on her brothers here is definitely sarcastic.

Edward and Fly went out yesterday very early in a couple of shooting jackets, and came home like a couple of bad shots, for they killed nothing at all. They are out again to-day, and are not yet returned. Delightful sport! They are just come home, Edward with his two brace, Frank with his two and a half. What amiable young men!

LETTER TO CASSANDRA, ROWLING, SEPTEMBER 15TH, 1796

HOW DO I COOK TO IMPRESS?

Q YOU'VE BEEN TASKED WITH COOKING DINNER FOR YOUR HUSBAND'S BOSS AND HIS WIFE FOR THE FIRST TIME EVER. AS YOU'VE NEVER EVEN HAD HIS WORK COLLEAGUES OVER FOR A MEAL, YOU'RE, QUITE FRANKLY, TERRIFIED. YOU WOULD LIKE TO PROJECT A LOW-KEY AND RELAXED, BUT ALSO SOPHISTICATED, IMAGE. WHAT KIND OF MEAL CAN YOU COOK TO ACHIEVE BOTH AND IMPRESS YOUR GUESTS?

 You don't need to be a good cook to be a Jane Austen heroine. Jane was able to leave a considerable amount of the domestic grind to her elder sister, but even Cassandra would not have spent hours in the kitchen; her role would have been more of an organizational and managerial one. Their friend, Martha Lloyd, came to live with them at Chawton and was a very practical addition to the home. Her recipe book is still at Jane Austen's House Museum, giving us a wonderful record of what the family ate, home remedies, and even the household's recipe for ink.

There was a balance between being involved and getting one's hands dirty. Mrs. Bennet is typically outraged when Mr. Collins suggests that her daughters might do the latter: "The dinner ... was highly admired; and he begged to know to which of his fair cousins the excellence of its cookery was owing. But here he was set right by Mrs. Bennet, who assured him with some asperity that they were very well able to keep a good cook, and that her daughters had nothing to do in the kitchen." *

Mr. and Mrs. Morland's surprise on being applied to by Mr. Tilney for their consent to his marrying their daughter was, for a few minutes, considerable ...

"Catherine would make a sad, heedless young housekeeper to be sure," was her mother's foreboding remark; but quick was the consolation of there being nothing like practice.

NORTHANGER ABBEY

If Jane were in your position, she would ask Martha Lloyd what she should do. You can do the same. Look at recipes from Martha's book for inspiration or seek out a Martha Lloyd-ish friend. † Ask her to come up with some possible menus and help you practice cooking them. Martha outlived Jane by many years. In a surviving portrait, she's wearing Jane's treasured topaz cross. It's a mark of how much Jane and Cassandra loved her.

As well as the kind of collection of recipes made by Martha, there were best-selling cookbooks, such as Maria Rundell's *A New System of Domestic Cookery*. This went through many editions on both sides of the Atlantic—she was the Barefoot Contessa or Martha Stewart of the era. Her book had suggestions for menus, as well as recipes and tips, such as "How To Preserve a Granary Floor From Insects and Weasels" and making "A Paste For Chapped Hands."

* *P&P*, Ch13. † Many of Martha Lloyd's recipes are included in Maggie Black and Deirdre Le Faye's *The Jane Austen Cookbook* (British Museum Press, London, 1995) and Laura Boyle's *Cooking With Jane Austen and Friends* (Trail Publishing, Co. Durham, 2010)

Dinner parties were set out in a way that we would find odd. A huge variety of dishes would be put on the table all at once, and the guests would choose what they wanted from an astonishing selection. Maria Rundell suggests dozens of dishes that could be used for each course. The first course might include a choice of soups, such as fish, turtle, or mock turtle, a selection of boiled, stewed, and roasted meats from all parts of all farm animals, then pies, pastries, rabbit or hare, ragouts and fricassées, and boiled or stewed vegetables. Some dishes would then be removed to make way for a second course, which might include game, shellfish, fish, various types of bird, vegetables stewed or in sauces, as well as asparagus, green beans, peas, spinach, pickled oysters, pasta, and all kinds of lovely sweet tarts, cheesecakes, mince pies, and puddings, all put on the table together. The extras (more vegetables, pickles, and sauces) were put on a side table and brought around by the servants. Even after this, there would be another course of fruit, olives, cheese, and sweets.

With this system, everybody was certain to get something that they liked to eat, and plenty of it, while avoiding dishes that they really didn't care for. If Martha Lloyd were helping you today, she'd think you were lucky to be able to offer so few dishes, but would still want to be sure that what you served looked beautiful, and that people didn't have to eat things that they hated.

Jane Austen doesn't give descriptions of food in her novels for the sake of it—it is always to tell us something about the host or the diners. In this scene at Pemberley, Elizabeth tastes how sweet life with Mr. Darcy might be: "The next variation which their visit afforded was produced by the entrance of servants with cold meat, cake, and a variety of all the finest fruits in season … There was now employment for the whole party—for though they could not all talk, they could all eat; and the beautiful pyramids of grapes, nectarines, and peaches soon collected them round the table."* Be sure that what you serve is beautiful and seems luxurious.

Martha Lloyd would advise you to cook whatever is seasonal. In Jane's time, most people would have had only what was in season and what had been preserved. This means eating what tastes right for the time of year and doesn't cost you a fortune. Here is Jane with her brother Edward and his family, stopping for dinner on their way to Bath in 1799. It's May and their seasonal food sounds delicious.

> *At Devizes we had comfortable rooms and a good dinner, to which we sat down about five; amongst other things we had asparagus and a lobster, which made me wish for you, and some cheesecakes, on which the children made so delightful a supper as to endear the town of Devizes to them for a long time.*
>
> LETTER TO CASSANDRA, BATH, MAY 17TH, 1799

* *P&P*, Ch45

HOW CAN I GET THE NEIGHBORHOOD EYESORE MOVED?

Q YOU LIVE IN A NICE AREA AND YOUR BUDDING FRIENDSHIP WITH THE WOMAN NEXT DOOR HAS BEEN GOING WELL—AT LEAST, IT WAS UNTIL SHE INSTALLED THE MOST HIDEOUS STATUE OF VENUS IMAGINABLE IN HER FRONT YARD. YOU'VE TRIED TO IGNORE IT, BUT THE FACT IS THAT EVERY TIME YOU LOOK OUT THE WINDOW, ALL YOU SEE IS BOTTICELLI'S WORST NIGHTMARE. CAN YOU GENTLY SUGGEST SHE TAKE THE STATUE DOWN, OR DO YOU HAVE TO LIVE WITH IT?

A Think of yourself as being like Mrs. Bennet with Lady Lucas as a neighbor (or perhaps the other way around): "Lady Lucas was a very good kind of woman, not too clever to be a valuable neighbor to Mrs. Bennet."*

Of course, you will be much cleverer than either of those two, but the thing to focus on is that they are friends, that Lady Lucas is good and kind, and a valuable neighbor to Mrs. Bennet. It would have been terribly sad if they had fallen out. We should imagine them remaining friends for evermore, trading cups of tea and boasts about the grandchildren. Jane Austen would advise you to focus on what you and your neighbor have in common, and one of those things is your love of gardens. Your friendship can continue to blossom, and you might also find a sneaky way to do away with this hideous statue.

P&P, Ch5

Change in a garden is rapid. Jane and Cassandra kept each other up to date with the interesting garden developments when one of them was away. This was written around two years after they had moved to Chawton—everything was starting to come up roses: "You cannot imagine—it is not in human nature to imagine—what a nice walk we have round the orchard. The row of beech look very well indeed, and so does the young quickset hedge in the garden. I hear to-day that an apricot has been detected on one of the trees." *

"This is pretty, very pretty," said Fanny, looking around her as they were thus sitting together one day; "every time I come into this shrubbery I am more struck with its growth and beauty. Three years ago, this was nothing but a rough hedgerow along the upper side of the field, never thought of as anything, or capable of becoming anything ..."

MANSFIELD PARK

Why not suggest some plants that would provide drapery for the goddess—she would look so much more beautiful that way—and climbers grow very fast. You could offer gardening books or share the advice of experts. Henry Crawford's services as an experienced improver of gardens are offered to Mr. Rushworth—an offer that poor Mr. Rushworth will regret accepting, although not because of the quality of the advice.

Jane would recommend the clever use of hedges and shrubs as screens. She found them delightful at Chawton and essential in her fiction; much can be concealed by them, but remember that wherever you are, things can still be overheard: "Anne, really tired herself, was glad to sit down; and she very soon heard Captain Wentworth and Louisa in the hedge-row behind her ... Louisa's voice was the first distinguished. She seemed to be in the middle of some eager speech." †

* Letter to Cassandra, Chawton, May 31st, 1811. † P, Ch10

HOW DO I CREATE A GARDEN WHEN I LACK TIME AND KNOWLEDGE?

Q YOU HAVE A GARDEN SPACE FOR THE FIRST TIME, AND YOU'D LIKE TO HAVE A GO AT CULTIVATING IT, BUT YOU'VE NEVER BEEN THE MOST PLANT-FRIENDLY PERSON. CONSIDERING THE LONG HOURS YOU SPEND WORKING, TIME IS AT A PREMIUM, TOO. REALLY, YOU JUST NEED A FEW TIPS AND TRICKS TO GET THINGS GOING, AND YOU'D LIKE WHAT YOU'LL EVENTUALLY GROW TO REQUIRE MINIMAL UPKEEP, BUT TO STILL BE SPECIAL. WHERE SHOULD YOU START?

A You must do what beginners have always done—ask the opinion of a more experienced gardener. As you work long hours, you'd be best advised to pay somebody to get things off to a good start. Go by recommendation and get quotes. This is just what the Austens did when they were setting to work on the garden of the Southampton home that Jane, Cassandra, and their mother were to share with Frank and his wife, Mary.

"Our garden is putting in order by a man who bears a remarkably good character, has a very fine complexion, and asks something less than the first."

I'd guess that the gardener's "very fine complexion" was a testament to his experience—he sounds weather-beaten rather than young and trendy. He knew his onions. In the same letter, Jane explains that: "The shrubs which border the gravel walk, he says, are only sweetbriar and roses, and the latter of an indifferent sort; we mean to get a few of a better kind, therefore, and at my own particular desire he procures us some syringas." *

* Letter to Cassandra, Southampton, February 8th, 1807

Jane loved syringas, doubtless because of their gorgeous looks and scent, but also because of a line from William Cowper's poem, *The Winter Walk at Noon*.

"I could not do without a syringa, for the sake of Cowper's line" (she wrote in the same February, 1807 letter). "We talk also of a laburnum. The border under the terrace wall is clearing away to receive currants and gooseberry bushes, and a spot is found very proper for raspberries."

This garden was being planned in February. Jane was anticipating summer in the same way as Cowper does in his poem. Thoughts of your garden will sustain you through the dark months in the same way. Try to pick the kind of plants that last—the kind that Jane chose—small trees, shrubs, fruit bushes, and perennials. Do what Jane did—think of plants that you know you love and love to eat, or that have happy associations for you. Why not start with syringas?

> But let the months go round, a few short months ...
> And all shall be restored. These naked shoots,
> Barren as lances, along which the wind
> Makes wintry music, sighing as it goes,
> Shall put their graceful foliage on again,
> And more aspiring, and with ampler spread,
> Shall boast new charms, and more than they have lost
> Then each, in its peculiar honours clad,
> Shall publish, even to the distant eye,
> Its family and tribe. Laburnum rich
> In streaming gold; syringa ivory-pure;
>
> FROM "THE WINTER WALK AT NOON" BY WILLIAM COWPER

LEISURE & TRAVEL

CHARACTERS IN JANE AUSTEN'S NOVELS ARE
OFTEN ON THE MOVE, MAKING VISITS OR
TOURING GRAND HOUSES. JANE HERSELF WAS
EXCESSIVELY FOND OF DANCING AND BALLS,
BUT SHE KNEW THE DOWNSIDE OF LEISURE:
TEDIOUS COMPANY, BAD WEATHER, AND
RAUCOUS CHILDREN. SHE HAS JUST AS MUCH
TO SAY ABOUT HAVING A GOOD TIME IN ONE'S
SPARE TIME AS SHE DOES ABOUT HAVING FUN
WITH BONNETS AND BILLETS-DOUX.

I NEED TO MAKE THE BEST OF BAD COMPANY. HELP!

 YOU CAN'T BE QUITE SURE HOW IT HAPPENED, BUT IT LOOKS LIKE YOU'RE SPENDING YOUR VACATION WITH THE MOST IRRITATING COUPLE ALIVE. THE CONSTANT BICKERING IS JUST THE TIP OF THE ICEBERG; EVEN WHEN THEY SEPARATE, YOU DON'T SEEM TO HAVE MUCH IN COMMON WITH EITHER OF THEM. DESPITE THAT, THIS IS YOUR ONE VACATION OF THE YEAR AND YOU'RE DETERMINED TO MAKE THE BEST OF IT. ARE THERE ANY TIPS TO MAKE SURE YOU HAVE A GOOD TIME?

 Oh dear—this is far from ideal. Are you sure that you cannot change the weeks that you are going? Perhaps you could even postpone your trip until next year and do something else instead. Plead work, plead anything! Your vacation company might well let you change your booking for a not too extortionate fee. First of all, try to follow the example of Elinor and Marianne Dashwood, who are resolute about not spending time with the appalling Palmers:

"'Oh! my dear Miss Dashwood,' said Mrs. Palmer soon afterwards, 'I have got such a favor to ask of you and your sister. Will you come and spend some time at Cleveland this Christmas? Now, pray do—and come while the Westons are with us. You cannot think how happy I shall be! It will be quite delightful!—My love,' applying to her husband, 'don't you long to have the Miss Dashwoods come to Cleveland?'

'Certainly'—he replied with a sneer—'I came into Devonshire with no other view.'

'There now'—said his lady, 'you see Mr. Palmer expects you; so you cannot refuse to come.'

Oh no—it's the Palmers!

*"...We do not live a great way from him in the country, you know,
—not above ten miles, I dare say."*
"Much nearer thirty," said her husband.
*"Ah! well! there is not much difference. I never was at his house;
but they say it is a sweet, pretty place."*
"As vile a spot as I ever saw in my life," said Mr. Palmer.

SENSE AND SENSIBILITY

They both eagerly and resolutely declined her invitation." *

If you absolutely do have to go at the same time as these people, you must, as you say, make the best of it. I don't think Jane would suggest asking this couple to stop being so tedious. You cannot make them get on, and intervening is inappropriate and likely to be pointless.

* *S&S*, Ch20

Only a highly-trained professional would have a hope of having any impact; your possible companions probably take pleasure in provoking each other, rather like the Bennets:

"'You take delight in vexing me.' [Mrs. Bennet tells her husband] 'You have no compassion on my poor nerves.'

'You mistake me, my dear. I have a high respect for your nerves. They are my old friends. I have heard you mention them with consideration these twenty years at least.'" *

Nobody would want to go on vacation with Mr. and Mrs. Bennet. It's hard to imagine them even going on vacation together. When their girls travel, it is with other people. Lizzy knows that she will have a wonderful vacation with her Aunt and Uncle Gardiner, and is overjoyed at the prospect: "'Oh! what hours of transport we shall spend! And when we *do* return, it shall not be like other travelers, without being able to give one accurate idea of anything. We *will* know where we have gone—we *will* recollect what we have seen. Lakes, mountains, and rivers shall not be jumbled together in our imaginations; nor, when we attempt to describe any particular scene, will we begin quarreling about its relative situation. Let *our* first effusions be less insupportable than those of the generality of travelers.'" †

So if you really can't change your plans and really are stuck with the

* *P&P*, Ch1. † *P&P*, Ch27

194

Bennets or the Palmers, try to find at least one of the Gardiners to come with you. If that also proves to be impossible, don't despair. You must seek out more sympathetic companions while you are away. In *Northanger Abbey*, Catherine Morland goes to Bath with Mr. and Mrs. Allen, who are kind, but not much fun and don't have much to say to her. Catherine throws herself into life in Bath, grasping every opportunity for fun and friendship. You must do that, too. You'll meet other people in similar situations to yours and you need not restrict yourself to doing things with your tedious fellow travelers. Be like Catherine, and go on walks, to the theater, and out dancing.

You may meet people as dreadful as Isabella and John Thorpe at first, but somewhere out there will be an Eleanor Tilney, an ideal friend, who is also in need of companionship. You may find that you meet a Henry Tilney, too. He and Catherine are in Bath for just a few short weeks together, but it turns out to be much more than a vacation romance.

Anybody who loves music as much as Jane Austen did would advise you to take a portable music device. Those headphones will be your friends, even if you can't find any others. Whatever you do, and whoever you go with, be certain to take plenty to read; when you need a vacation from your vacation, a good book will be the answer. As Catherine Morland puts it: "'... while I have *Udolpho* to read, I feel as if nobody could make me miserable.'" *

> *The employment of mind and dissipation of unpleasant ideas which only reading could produce made her thankfully turn to a book.*
>
> THE WATSONS

* NA, Ch6

WHAT MAKES A BETTER VACATION: RELAXATION OR CULTURE?

 YOU FINALLY MANAGED TO GET A FULL WEEK OFF FROM YOUR BUSY JOB AND AFTER PINCHING YOUR PENNIES YOU'VE SAVED UP ENOUGH MONEY FOR A DECENT VACATION. BUT NOW YOU CAN'T DECIDE WHAT TO DO: DO YOU SPEND A WEEK RESTING ON A TROPICAL BEACH SOMEWHERE, UNFETTERED BY THE RAT RACE OF CITY LIFE? OR DO YOU JET OFF TO A VIBRANT EUROPEAN CITY TO TAKE IN THE SIGHTS AND SOUNDS OF LIVING ART AND HISTORY?

Jane Austen would have wanted to do it all. People sometimes think of her as having led a quiet and uneventful life, but although she was a clergyman's daughter and lived mostly in rural Hampshire, she also spent significant amounts of time in London, Bath, Southampton (which was then a thriving spa resort), and at the seaside. She stayed with her rich relatives in Kent, corresponded with the Price Regent's Private Secretary, and went to plenty of sparkling parties. She loved the theater, and when she stayed in London with her brother Henry and his glamorous wife, Eliza, it was often just off Covent Garden. The house is still there today.

"Here I am once more in this scene of dissipation and vice, and I begin already to find my morals corrupted ..." she joked in a letter to Cassandra in August 1796.* The letter continued that they were going to Astley's that night—an equestrian circus near Westminster Bridge.

> *I had great amusement among the pictures; and the driving about, the carriage being open, was very pleasant. I liked my solitary elegance very much, and was ready to laugh all the time at my being where I was. I could not but feel that I had naturally small right to be parading about London in a barouche.*
>
> LETTER TO CASSANDRA, LONDON, MAY 24TH, 1813

Jane was still enjoying stays in London nearly twenty years later. After a morning's shopping, she and Henry went to the Society of Painters in Oil and Water Colours Exhibition in Spring Gardens, where she tried to spot likenesses of her characters.

"I was very well pleased ... with a small portrait of Mrs. Bingley, excessively like her. I went in hopes of seeing one of her sister, but there was no Mrs. Darcy. Perhaps, however, I may find her in the great exhibition, which we shall go to if we have time .... Mrs. Bingley's is exactly herself—size, shaped face, features, and sweetness; there never was a greater likeness. She is dressed in a white gown, with green ornaments, which convinces me of what I had always supposed, that green was a favorite color with her. I dare say Mrs. D. will be in yellow." †

* Letter to Cassandra, London, August 23rd, 1796. † Letter to Cassandra, London, May 24th, 1813

We know that she had some high times by the coast as well, and Sidmouth, Dawlish, Lyme Regis, Weymouth, Cromer, Southend, Ramsgate, and, of course, Brighton all feature in her work. The seaside, in Jane's time, as now, was often a place of seduction and romance, and this is reflected in her fiction. If only *Sanditon* had been finished, we'd have had a whole seaside novel. Jane was interested in seeing new places and how old ones were changing.

The new Mr. and Mrs. Knightley set off for a "fortnight absence in a tour to the seaside" * on their honeymoon. Emma has never seen the sea—and that's where I think Jane's advice to you would begin. Why not do something that you haven't done before or something that will make the most enjoyable contrast to what your day-to-day life is now?

Jane was devastated when she first heard that she had to quit her childhood home in the countryside and move to Bath, but by the time of the move, a complete change of scenery seemed to appeal: "I get more and more reconciled to the idea of our removal. We have lived long enough in this neighborhood: the Basingstoke balls are certainly on the decline, there is something interesting in the bustle of going away, and the prospect of spending future summers by the sea or in Wales is very delightful." †

* E, Ch55. † Letter to Cassandra, Steventon, January 3rd, 1801

But after spending a few years in Bath, she left with "happy feelings of escape." * Close your eyes and picture yourself on first one kind of vacation, then the other. Which would give you the happiest feelings of escape? That is the one to choose.

The other thing to keep in mind is the season when you'll be going. Anne Elliot wants to put off her trip to the city because she is "dreading the possible heats of September in all the white glare of Bath" and doesn't want to "forego all the influence so sweet and so sad of the autumnal months in the country." †

In just the same way, you might want to avoid a trip to a European capital when it will be baking hot, horribly dusty, and crowded with backpackers; but there again you might be like Anne's friend, Lady Russell: "Everybody has their taste in noises as well as in other matters; and sounds are quite innoxious, or most distressing, by their sort rather than their quantity. When Lady Russell, not long afterwards, was entering Bath on a wet afternoon, and driving through the long course of streets from the Old Bridge to Camden Place, amidst the dash of other carriages, the heavy rumble of carts and drays, the bawling of newsmen, muffin-men, and milk-men, and the ceaseless clink of pattens, she made no complaint. No, these were noises which belonged to the winter pleasures: her spirits rose under their influence … Anne did not share these feelings." ‡

Whatever you choose, make sure it will be what suits you (and not Lady Russell) best. Try to feel that you have every right to be there, just as Jane had every right to be parading around London in solitary elegance in that fancy and fashionable barouche.

Have a wonderful vacation!

HELP! THE SUMMER VACATION HAS STARTED AND THE KIDS ARE CAUSING MAYHEM ALREADY.

Q IT'S THAT TIME OF YEAR AGAIN; THE SUMMER VACATION IS HERE AND THE KIDS ARE HOME FOR WEEKS ON END. YOU LOVE HAVING THEM AROUND, OF COURSE, BUT THE NATIVES ARE GETTING RESTLESS AND IN DIRE NEED OF ENTERTAINMENT—PREFERABLY BEFORE THEY START DESTROYING THE HOUSE AND EVERYTHING IN IT OUT OF SHEER BOREDOM. WHAT CAN YOU DO TO DISTRACT THEM FROM DESTRUCTIVE INTENT?

A When you have a house full of children, it's tempting to hide and hope they'll just start amusing themselves—well, they might—but they might drive you and each other crazy, too.

Jane often had children with her. In October 1808, two nephews came to stay with her in Southampton because their mother had just died. Cassandra was away being a kind sister and aunt to their relatives in Kent. Teenage boys who have just lost their mother can't be the easiest house guests, but Jane proved herself to be the ideal aunt. Letters show how she immediately set to work, making sure that the boys recovered from their journey. (They were freezing; being typical teenagers, they'd chosen to ride on the outside of the coach.) She devoted herself to caring for them without smothering. Their father's "letter was read over by each of them yesterday, and with many tears; George sobbed aloud, Edward's tears do not flow so easily ..." *

* Letter to Cassandra, Southampton, October 24th, 1808

She knew that she had to balance keeping them busy with giving them space to grieve, and their stay was filled with games, trips on the water, walks by the sea, and time to think and read.

"While I write now," she told Cassandra, "George is most industriously making and naming paper ships, at which he afterwards shoots with horse-chestnuts brought from Steventon on purpose; and Edward equally intent over the 'Lake of Killarney,' [a novel] twisting himself about in one of our great chairs ..." *

Jane knew that if you have children or young people in the house with nothing to do, they'll get bored and miserable. None of their activities and excursions would have cost much—most would have been free. She kept things up her sleeve—particular card games, interesting trips—so that when spirits were flagging, there was something else to do. She made sure that they all kept getting outside. Life in Southampton would have had its particular interests and the house was right beside the water, so they could easily launch those paper ships. Bilbocatch, at which George was "indefatigable," is cup and ball—sometimes it's about finding something that will become a craze.

She tailored activities to whomever her visitor was. Imagine being this little girl: "... she is now talking away at my side and examining the treasures of my writing-desk drawers—very happy, I believe." †

If you want to have happy vacations, do what Jane did—find the right combination of games, books, and trips outdoors.

> *We do not want amusement: bilbocatch, at which George is indefatigable; spillikins, paper ships, riddles, conundrums, and cards, with watching the flow and ebb of the river, and now and then a stroll out, keep us well employed ...*
>
> LETTER TO CASSANDRA,
> SOUTHAMPTON,
> OCTOBER 24TH, 1808

* Letter to Cassandra, Southampton, October 24th, 1808. † Ibid.

POTENTIAL DEATH-TRAP OR A VOLVO?

 YOU'VE HEARD SOME PRETTY HORRIFIC THINGS SAID ABOUT MOTORCYCLE ACCIDENTS, AND MORE THAN ONCE YOUR MOM HAS THREATENED TO DISOWN YOU IF YOU EVER GOT ON ONE OF THOSE DEATH MACHINES, BUT THE FACT IS YOU KIND OF LIKE THEM ... AND YOU ARE CONSIDERING BUYING ONE. NOW THAT YOU'RE OLD ENOUGH AND YOUR MOM NO LONGER HAS A HOLD OVER YOU FINANCIALLY, YOU'RE FREE TO DECIDE FOR YOURSELF. SHOULD YOU BE SEXY AND DANGEROUS AND GO WITH THE BIKE, OR BUY A CAR TO BE SENSIBLE AND SAFE?

When the boorish John Thorpe makes his entrance in *Northanger Abbey*, it's at top speed. He's driving a gig, and he nearly knocks Catherine Morland and his sister, Isabella, down. It's as though he screeches to a halt as "the horse was immediately checked with a violence which almost threw him on his haunches." * He's like Mr. Toad but without the money or the stately home. Strangely enough, Catherine isn't wooed by his boasts of how fast he drives. The conversation about routes and mileage leaves her cold, too. If you want to buy a motorcycle, be careful that you don't turn into John Thorpe—it won't win you any friends and you might well kill somebody.

A gig was a small, light carriage, pulled by a single horse. It was nippy, but at the cheaper end of the market, and didn't have a cover so was not always practical. John Thorpe would probably have preferred an actual curricle, which was drawn by two horses so a little more upmarket and with the bonus of a hood. It was more like a modern small convertible—perhaps that's the way you should go.

* *NA*, Ch7

John Thorpe starts boasting:

"Curricle-hung, you see; seat, trunk, sword case, splashing board, lamps, silver molding, all you see complete; the ironwork as good as new, or better. He asked fifty guineas; I closed with him directly, threw down the money, and the carriage was mine."

NORTHANGER ABBEY

It wasn't that owning a gig was shameful, just that a curricle was superior. Willoughby drove one. They could also tip over easily, so he was showing off when he drove off really fast in his. We get hints of Willoughby and Thorpe's untrustworthy natures from their driving and their attitudes to taking women out with them. Catherine Morland and Marianne Dashwood make themselves vulnerable by being driven out alone by these men.

Thorpe lets on that the purchase of his gig wasn't even a considered one: "'I had pretty well determined on a curricle too; but I chanced to meet him on Magdalen Bridge, as he was driving into Oxford, last term: 'Ah! Thorpe,' said he, 'do you happen to want such a little thing as this? It is a capital one of the kind, but I am cursed tired of it.' 'Oh! D——,' said I; 'I am your man; what do you ask?' And how much do you think he did, Miss Morland?'" *

Jane would tell you to steer clear of impulse buys.

Catherine has a dreadful time out driving with Thorpe. He exaggerates everything, boasting about how well he controls his horse, although Catherine can't help but notice that "the animal continued to go on in the same quiet manner, without showing the smallest propensity towards any unpleasant vivacity." †

Being driven by Henry Tilney is a different matter for her. Henry is quietly confident and skillful: "... so different from the only gentleman–coachman whom it was in her power to compare him with! And then his hat sat so well, and the innumerable capes of his greatcoat looked so becomingly important! To be driven by him, next to being dancing with him, was certainly the greatest happiness in the world." ‡

If a Georgian gentleman was extremely rich and wanted to impress, then he might choose a barouche. This is what Henry Crawford drives in *Mansfield Park*. It was drawn by four horses, but was much more impressive and more fun than a coach (the equivalent of a family car, as owned by the Bennets). A barouche could carry up to six people. The driver and a companion could sit at the front (slightly secluded so ideal for flirting) with four people behind, facing each other in pairs. Barouches were like ridiculously expensive convertibles.

In *Emma,* the only type of carriage specifically named is the Sucklings' barouche-landau. Elsewhere in the novel, we only hear about "carriages" (the generic term)

* *NA*, Ch7. † *NA*, Ch10. ‡ *NA*, Ch20

because Jane wanted to make such a joke of Mrs. Elton's boasting about how rich her brother-in-law is. A barouche-landau was a status symbol that really turned heads, but it sounds as though you are more in the market for a curricle.

I don't think that Jane would ever advise you to forget about safety. She lost Jane Cooper, a much-loved cousin, to a carriage accident, and another dear friend, Anne Lefroy, to a riding accident. The roads then, as now, were dangerous and fatalities were common. You can't forget the vagaries of how *other* people will drive. Perhaps the choice you are making shouldn't be between sexy and dangerous or sensible and safe. Henry Tilney manages to be sexy *and* safe. Jane knew that it isn't just about what you drive, it's the way that you drive it.

… she found herself with Henry in the curricle, as happy a being as ever existed. A very short trial convinced her that a curricle was the prettiest equipage in the world … Henry drove so well—so quietly—without making any disturbance, without parading to her, or swearing …

NORTHANGER ABBEY

HOW CAN WE VACATION WITH A FUSSY FRIEND?

 SINCE THE DAY YOU MET, YOU AND YOUR FRIENDS HAVE BEEN TALKING ABOUT GOING AWAY SOMEWHERE TOGETHER FOR A LUXURIOUS BREAK. THAT WAS NEARLY FIFTEEN YEARS AGO, BUT YOU'VE FINALLY AGREED THE TIME IS NOW. UNFORTUNATELY, OVER THE YEARS, ONE MEMBER OF YOUR GROUP HAS BECOME A FUSSPOT. SHE DOES NOTHING BUT FRET ABOUT FOOD AND HER (SEEMINGLY IMAGINARY) AILMENTS. NOT ONLY THIS, BUT SHE TRIES TO PERSUADE YOU ALL TO FOLLOW WHICHEVER CRAZY DIET SHE'S ON. YOU DON'T WANT TO EXCLUDE HER, BUT HOW CAN YOU STOP HER MOANING AND FUSSING FROM RUINING IT FOR EVERYBODY?

 Jane Austen's seaside Sanditon might be the perfect place for you and your friends to go. It's a tragedy that Jane died before she could finish this novel, and it was typical of her to be working on a novel about hypochondriacs when her own health was so bad. Jane spent about three months on it, but then had to abandon it because she was too ill to carry on. During this period, she was at home in Chawton, deep in the Hampshire countryside; I've often wondered if she was longing for the sea while she was writing it.

Jane was a vigorous person—as well as walking, she loved bathing in the sea: "The Bathing was so delightful this morning & Molly so pressing with me to enjoy myself that I believe I staid in rather too long …" *

Swimming in the sea was hugely popular, and people believed that the bracing cold water during the winter months would give the greatest health benefits.

* Letter to Cassandra, Lyme, September 14th, 1804

Diana Parker complains:

"We have consulted physician after physician in vain, till we are quite convinced that they can do nothing for us and that we must trust to our own knowledge of our own wretched constitutions for any relief."

SANDITON

"The sea air and sea bathing together were nearly infallible, one or the other of them being a match for every disorder of the stomach, the lungs or the blood. They were antispasmodic, antipulmonary, antiseptic, antibillious, and antirheumatic. Nobody could catch cold by the sea; nobody wanted appetite by the sea; nobody wanted spirits; nobody wanted strength." *

* S, Ch2

Your friend would have felt at home in Sanditon, set on the Sussex coast. She could have made friends with Susan and Diana Parker and compared ailments with them. An Austen vacation would have been to Bath, a spa resort, or the seaside. Choosing somewhere like that should meet everybody's needs, and your friend will be in heaven. If other people are being paid to be nice to her and listen to her moaning, the rest of you won't have to. The spa treatments can fill her time so that she doesn't drive the rest of you crazy.

When Jane was in Bath and by the seaside it was not primarily for her own health. Her brother Edward's more often gave concern: "Edward has not been well these last two days; his appetite has failed him, and he has complained of sick and uncomfortable feelings, which, with other symptoms, make us think of the gout … He made an important purchase yesterday: no less so than a pair of coach-horses …" *

Jane would have looked on any imaginary ailments in the same way as the level-headed heroine of *Sanditon*, Charlotte Heywood. She probably put some of the words that she wanted to say into Charlotte's mouth: "As far as I can understand what nervous complaints are, I have a great idea of the efficacy of air and exercise for them—daily, regular exercise—and I should recommend rather more of it to *you* than I suspect you are in the habit of taking." †

Emma Woodhouse also has to find ways to navigate other people's hypochondria and fussiness. You will have to do the same so that your annoying friend can't dictate what you all eat and drink. Make sure you stay somewhere that can cater for her,

* Letter to Cassandra, Bath, June 19th, 1799. † *S*, Ch10

but where she won't be able to impose her strictures on you. If you don't, it might be a bit like dining with the Parker sisters, who worry about the strength of other people's cocoa, or Mr. Woodhouse, who warns against eating cake. His excessive concern for everybody meant that Emma often had to quietly intervene to make sure that people had enough to eat and enough that was nice.

Be like Charlotte and Emma, and don't let the Parker sisters or Mr. Woodhouse take over. Here is Mr. Woodhouse, looking after his guests: "'Mrs. Bates, let me propose your venturing on one of these eggs. An egg boiled very soft is not unwholesome. Serle understands boiling an egg better than anybody. I would not recommend an egg boiled by anybody else; but you need not be afraid, they are very small ... let Emma help you to a *little* bit of tart—a *very* little bit ... I do not advise the custard. Mrs. Goddard, what say you to *half* a glass of wine? A *small* half-glass, put into a tumbler of water? I do not think it could disagree with you.'" *

Your friend may well be like Frank Churchill's aunt, whose illnesses and fancies governed her family. But if you manage everything in advance, you'll still be able to have a lovely time. Who knows, your friend may decide at the last minute that she is too ill to come. Be nice to her, however, just in case it turns out there really is something wrong ...

WHAT SHOULD MY BOOK CLUB READ?

Q ONE THING YOU NEVER SEEM TO FIND THE TIME FOR THESE DAYS IS READING. AS YOU WERE A BOOKWORM WHEN YOU WERE YOUNGER, YOU HAVE DECIDED TO START A CLUB IN ORDER TO GET BACK TO BASICS AND TAKE SOME TIME TO IMPROVE YOUR MIND. BUT YOUR GROUP IS MADE UP OF SOME VERY DIFFERENT PEOPLE WITH VERY DIFFERENT TASTES. SO HOW DO YOU CHOOSE WHICH KIND OF BOOKS TO READ?

> *"I have received a very civil note from Mrs. Martin, requesting my name as a subscriber to her library ... As an inducement to subscribe, Mrs. Martin tells me that her collection is not to consist only of novels, but of every kind of literature, &c. She might have spared this pretension to our family, who are great novel-readers and not ashamed of being so ..."*
>
> LETTER TO CASSANDRA, STEVENTON, DECEMBER 18TH, 1798

A Jane Austen would advise you to steer clear of any dull nonfiction. When she was going to stay with her best friend, Martha, she joked: "You distress me cruelly by your request about books. I cannot think of any to bring with me ... I come to you to be talked to, not to read or hear reading; I can do *that* at home; and indeed I am now laying in a stock of intelligence to pour out on you as *my* share of the conversation. I am reading Henry's *History of England*, which I will repeat to you in any manner you may prefer, either in a loose, desultory, unconnected stream, or dividing my recital, as the historian divides it himself, into seven parts:—The Civil and Military: Religion: Constitution: Learning and Learned Men: Arts and Sciences: Commerce, Coins, and Shipping: and Manners. So that for every evening in the week there will be a different subject . . ." *

She suggests that Martha does her part by "repeating the French Grammar." So that's what not to do. Avoid anything boring and avoid things that will encourage people to be boring. Book clubs are meant to be amusing.

You should definitely be favoring novels. Catherine Morland and Isabella Thorpe in *Northanger Abbey* have a love of novels in common. Isabella gives Catherine a list for her delectation—they are all truly "horrid"—they'd be read for the thrill of being scared: "'I will read you their names directly; here they are, in my pocketbook. *Castle of Wolfenbach*, *Clermont*, *Mysterious Warnings*, *Necromancer of the Black Forest*, *Midnight Bell*, *Orphan of the Rhine*, and *Horrid Mysteries*. Those will last us some time.'" †

* Letter to Martha Lloyd, Steventon, November 12th, 1800. † *NA*, Ch6

These were actual novels, and Jane's earliest readers would have been able to read them and know what the list said about Isabella and her somewhat trashy tastes. Jane was an omnivorous reader, but I don't think she would recommend starting with one of them. In *Northanger Abbey,* she endorsed *Cecilia* and *Camilla* by Frances Burney and *Belinda* by Maria Edgeworth.

Even the title *Pride and Prejudice* was taken from the final chapter of *Cecilia*: "Yet this, however, remember: if to PRIDE AND PREJUDICE you owe your miseries, so wonderfully is good and evil balanced, that to PRIDE AND PREJUDICE you will also owe their termination." *

When Frances Burney's *Camilla* came out in 1796, one of the subscribers was "Miss J. Austen, Steventon." Subscribing here meant committing to buy a copy— it was more than just preordering on Amazon, but shows the same eager anticipation. Maria Edgeworth's *Belinda* (another novel that Jane enjoyed) was first published in 1801. It predates the publication of Jane's first novels, although not their composition. The heroine is "handsome, graceful, sprightly, and accomplished"— sound familiar?

Although Jane might recommend novels of her own time and earlier, she'd say that you should also read things that have just been published. One of the joys of a book club is discovering new publications.

Book groups are not a new phenomenon. There were growing numbers of libraries and reading groups during Jane's time. Books were expensive, so it made sense to borrow and share. Jane read widely and from her own experience would advise you to keep an open mind about other people's choices of

* Burney, F. (2008)

books. While Cassandra was away, she kept her up to date about the doings of their own Chawton Book Society: "We quite run over with books … I am reading a Society octavo, an 'Essay on the Military Police and Institutions of the British Empire' by Capt. Pasley of the Engineers, a book which I protested against at first, but which upon trial I find delightfully written and highly entertaining …" *

> As the lovely Henry Tilney puts it:
> *"The person, be it gentleman or lady, who has not pleasure in a good novel, must be intolerably stupid."*
> NORTHANGER ABBEY

Jane preferred an octavo-size book to a much larger, more old-fashioned quarto one.† This could be another of your guiding principles—nothing too big.

However, Jane wasn't always as tolerant of her fellow readers as perhaps she could have been. She looked down her nose at the Steventon and Manydown Society nearby where the ladies read "those enormous great stupid thick quarto volumes … Capt. Pasley's book is too good for their Society. They will not understand a man who condenses his thoughts into an octavo." ‡ But she would urge you to try to make allowances for some of your members: "Your Aunt C. does not like desultory novels …" Jane told her niece Anna, who was writing a novel and looking for guidance in August 1814. §

Your club's first choice is important. You could start with *Northanger Abbey*. It is certainly not desultory, and is a novel about novels, so should get you talking about reading and please everybody you'd like to keep as a member of your book club.

* Letter to Cassandra, Chawton, January 24th, 1813.
† Book sizes were named according to the number of leaves (double-sided pages) created from the original large sheets of paper used during the printing and binding process. A "folio" was very big—the sheet had been cut in half to make just two leaves. A "quarto" was made with leaves that were each a quarter of the original sheet, while the smaller, handier "octavo" was made by printing and cutting the sheet to make eight leaves.
‡ Letter to Cassandra, Chawton, February 9th, 1813. § Letter to Anna Austen, Chawton, August 18th, 1814

CHARACTER SUMMARIES

SENSE AND SENSIBILITY
First published: 1811

Miss Elinor Dashwood: Level-headed eldest of the three Dashwood sisters. In love with Edward Ferrars; is she just too sensible?

Miss Marianne Dashwood: The middle one; wildly romantic; is swept off her feet by Willoughby.

Miss Margaret Dashwood: Their little sister.

Mr. James Willoughby: The hero, or not all that he seems?

Mr. Edward Ferrars: Brother of the horrible Fanny Dashwood (née Ferrars); in love with Elinor but secretly engaged to Lucy Steele.

Mr. Robert Ferrars: Vain and shallow brother of Edward and Fanny.

Mrs. Ferrars: Mean mother of Edward, Robert and Fanny. She's determined that her sons will marry well and Edward is worried about displeasing her.

Miss Lucy Steele: Successful schemer; is holding Edward to a boyish promise to marry her.

Miss Anne Steele: Lucy's older sister; obsessed by beaux; not very bright.

Colonel Brandon: An older man in love with Marianne but biding his time.

Mrs. Fanny Dashwood: Wife of Elinor and Marianne's half-brother, **John**; she's greedy and selfish.

Sir John Middleton and Lady Mary Middleton: Friendly owners of Barton Park; they offer Barton Cottage to Elinor and Marianne's mother.

Mr. Thomas and Mrs. Charlotte Palmer: Charlotte is Lady Middleton's sister. Thomas is standing for Parliament. He despises his wife. Theirs isn't a healthy marriage.

Mrs. Jennings: Cheery mother of Mrs. Palmer and Lady Middleton; takes Elinor and Marianne to London.

PRIDE AND PREJUDICE
First published: 1813

Mrs. Bennet: Desperate to find husbands for her five daughters because Mr. Collins will inherit Longbourn, their family home.

Mr. Bennet: He hasn't set aside enough money to help his daughters marry well or sorted out the inheritance problem.

The Miss Bennets (in age order):
Jane: Sweet-natured.
Elizabeth: Sparkling.
Mary: Priggish.
Kitty: Easily-led.
Lydia: Extrovert flirt (to put it politely).

The Reverend Mr. Collins: Obsequious clergyman cousin of Mr. Bennet; he is employed by Lady Catherine de Bourgh, Mr. Darcy's aunt.

Mr. Charles Bingley: A very eligible bachelor who moves into the neighborhood, bringing his spiteful sisters, **Miss Caroline Bingley** and **Mrs. Louisa Hurst**, with him. Falls in love with Jane Bennet.

Mr. Fitzwilliam Darcy: The most eligible bachelor; owner of Pemberley.

Miss Georgiana Darcy: Younger sister of Fitzwilliam, with a fortune of her own.

Mr. George Wickham: A militia officer and scoundrel who has tried to seduce Georgiana.

Miss Charlotte Lucas: Elizabeth's friend; she will settle for Mr. Collins.

Lady Catherine de Bourgh: Mr. Darcy's domineering aunt; she wants him to marry her sickly daughter, **Anne.**

Mr. and Mrs. Gardiner: The Bennet girls' sensible and kindly uncle and aunt.

MANSFIELD PARK
First published: 1814

Miss Fanny Price: Shy heroine; the Cinderella cousin of the Bertrams.

Lady Bertram: Indolent sister of Fanny's mother; devoted to her couch and her pug, but Fanny loves her anyway.

Sir Thomas Bertram: Fanny's rich uncle; attends to his estates in Antigua, but fails to notice what's rotten at home.

The Bertram Children:
Tom: Dissolute heir.
Edmund: Future clergyman secretly worshipped by Fanny.
Maria: Engaged to Mr. Rushworth because there was nobody else around; easily tempted.
Julia: Aspiring flirt.

Mrs. Norris: Fanny's poisonous aunt.

Dr. Grant: *Bon viveur;* current parson at Mansfield Park.

Mrs. Grant: Wife of Dr. G. and half-sister of Mary and Henry Crawford.

Mr. Henry Crawford: Clever, extremely eligible bachelor with plans to collect hearts.

Miss Mary Crawford: Henry's gorgeous, cynical, and equally unprincipled sister; Edmund falls in love with her.

Mr. Rushworth: Rich and stupid fiancé of Maria Bertram; one has to feel sorry for him.

The Hon. John Yates: Tom Bertram's friend; the bringer of theatrical misrule to Mansfield Park.

Mr. William Price: Fanny's sailor brother.

Mr. and Mrs. Price: Fanny's far-from-ideal parents.

Miss Susan Price: The heroine's younger sister; Fanny spots her great potential.

EMMA
First published: 1816

Miss Emma Woodhouse: Handsome, rich, and clever, Emma is mistress of Hartfield where she lives with her father.

Miss Harriet Smith: Sweet and suggestible; Emma persuades her to turn down an offer of marriage from **Robert Martin**.

Mr. Henry Woodhouse: Emma's fretful father; worries desperately about everybody's welfare.

Mr. George Knightley: The gentlemanly owner of the neighboring Donwell Abbey. It takes a while for Mr. Knightley and Emma to realize that they are in love.

Mrs. Anne Weston (formerly Miss Taylor): Emma's former governess, now married to the affable **Mr. Weston**. She is Emma's close friend and acted as a mother figure.

Miss Bates: Lives in reduced circumstances with her mother, **Mrs. Bates**, a good friend of Mr. Woodhouse. She adores her niece, Jane Fairfax.

Mrs. Isabella Knightley (née Woodhouse): Emma's older sister, now married to **Mr. Knightley's** brother, **John.** They have five children.

Mr. Frank Churchill: Mr. Weston's son by his first marriage; he has been brought up by his late mother's side of the family and has taken their name. He is secretly engaged to Jane Fairfax.

Miss Jane Fairfax: Elegant and accomplished niece of Miss Bates; because she has no money she is destined to become a governess.

The Reverend Mr. Philip Elton: Socially ambitious vicar of Highbury.

Mrs. Augusta Elton (née Hawkins): Mr. Elton's new wife is loathed by Emma; she has lots of money but no taste.

NORTHANGER ABBEY
First published: 1818, posthumously

Miss Catherine Morland: Our heroine; she's trusting, friendly, and enthusiastic.

Mr. Henry Tilney: The hero; he reads, he dances, he's fun, and he will eventually stand up to his father in order to be with Catherine. He's older than her and likes to tease her.

General Tilney: Widower and despotic owner of Northanger Abbey.

Mr. James Morland: Brother of Catherine; he falls for Isabella Thorpe.

Miss Isabella Thorpe: Horrible flirt and false friend of Catherine.

Mr. John Thorpe: Boorish brother of Isabella; thinks Catherine should be in love with him.

Miss Eleanor Tilney: Elegant sister of Henry and ideal friend for Catherine; Miss Tilney always wears white.

Captain Tilney: More worldly brother of Henry and Eleanor; flirts with Isabella Thorpe.

Mr. and Mrs. Allen: Well-meaning neighbors of the Morland family who take Catherine with them to Bath; Mr. Allen has gout, Mrs. Allen loves frocks.

PERSUASION
First published: 1818, posthumously

Miss Anne Elliot: Steadfast heroine; was persuaded to break things off with Frederick Wentworth and now must let him know that she still loves him.

Captain Frederick Wentworth: Heartbroken by Anne; has now made his fortune at sea and is looking for a wife.

Sir Walter Elliot: Anne's father; he's so vain, he probably thinks the novel's about him. Has overspent so much that Kellynch Hall has to be rented out.

Miss Elizabeth Elliot: Vain older sister of Anne; her father's favorite.

Mary and Charles Musgrove: Mary is Anne and Elizabeth's needy younger sister; she uses Anne for unpaid child-minding duties. Anne turned Charles down because she still loved Frederick.

Lady Russell: Friend of Anne's late mother and dispenser of well-intentioned advice to Anne and her family.

Mrs. Penelope Clay: Freckled friend of Elizabeth; has designs on Sir Walter.

Mr. William Elliot: Heir presumptive to Sir Walter; he has designs on Anne as a way of securing the whole Elliot estate.

Admiral Croft: Sensible and friendly brother-in-law of Captain Wentworth; becomes the tenant of Kellynch Hall, thus bringing Captain Wentworth back into Anne's life.

Mrs. Sophia Croft: Sister of Captain Wentworth and wife of Admiral Croft. The Crofts show Anne how well marriages can work, even naval ones.

Miss Louisa Musgrove: High-spirited sister of Charles Musgrove. Sets her cap at Captain Wentworth but loses her footing on The Cobb at Lyme. She eventually finds love with another previously heartbroken sailor, Captain Benwick.

Miss Henrietta Musgrove: Sister of Charles and Louisa. Meant to be engaged to **Rev. Charles Hayter**, but could easily be lured away by a more eligible bachelor, Captain Wentworth, for instance.

Captain Harville: Hospitable friend of Captain Wentworth. Lives in Lyme with his wife and children after being wounded in action.

Mrs. Smith: Old school friend of Anne's with insider information on the true character of William Elliot.

THE WATSONS
First published: 1871, unfinished

The Reverend Mr. Watson: Widowed father of the heroine and her five siblings.

Miss Emma Watson: Our heroine. Emma has been brought up by a wealthy aunt but has to return to her immediate family when that aunt remarries.

Lord Osborne: Owner of Osborne Castle, Dorking; he is quite taken with Emma.

Mr. Tom Musgrave: Ambitious friend of Lord Osborne; seems a good prospect to Emma's husband-hunting sisters.

The Reverend Mr. Howard: The former tutor of Lord Osborne. Jane Austen told Cassandra that after Emma Watson had declined a proposal from Lord Osborne, she would marry him.

Master Charles Blake: A rare example of a nice child in Jane Austen's work; he loves to dance and Emma Watson dances with him.

SANDITON
First published: 1925, unfinished

Miss Charlotte Heywood: The sensible heroine and eldest Heywood daughter still at home.

Lady Denham: Landowner, grand lady of the neighborhood and Mr. Thomas Parker's collaborator in trying to develop Sanditon as a seaside resort.

Miss Clara Brereton: Elegant and astute poor relation and companion of Lady Denham.

Mr. Thomas Parker: Enthusiastic developer of Sanditon; sprains his ankle in a minor carriage accident and is taken in by the Heywood family. He invites Charlotte to Sanditon to say thank you.

Miss Diana and Miss Susan Parker: Hypochondriac sisters of Thomas, Sidney, and Arthur.

Mr. Arthur Parker: The youngest of the Parker siblings; rather flabby and certainly not as ill as his sisters fancy.

Mr. Sidney Parker: A different kind of Parker—he's good looking with "a decided air of ease and fashion, and a lively countenance."

Sir Edward Denham: Lady Denham's nephew by her second marriage; a probable villain.

BIOGRAPHY OF JANE

JANE AUSTEN WAS BORN IN STEVENTON, HAMPSHIRE, ON DECEMBER 16TH, 1775. SHE WAS THE SEVENTH OF EIGHT CHILDREN OF THE REVEREND GEORGE AUSTEN AND HIS NOBLY BORN WIFE, CASSANDRA LEIGH. HER PARENTS WERE CLEVER AND LOVING, BUT NOT RICH.

James (1765–1819), their firstborn, studied at Oxford, wrote poetry, and became a clergyman, following in his father's footsteps as Rector of Steventon. His daughter Anna (1793–1872) was one of Jane's favorite nieces and Jane advised her on writing novels. Anna's recollections, along with those of James Edward (1798–1874) and Caroline (1805–1880), her half siblings, have been invaluable to generations of fans.

Not much is known about **George** (1766–1838), who was disabled, probably deaf and with epilepsy. The Austens paid for him to lodge with a local family.

Edward (1767–1852) was adopted by rich, childless relatives and took their surname, Knight. He inherited the Godmersham estate in Kent and the Chawton estate in Hampshire. He had eleven children, including Fanny, another favorite niece of Jane's.

Henry (1771–1850) was probably Jane's favorite brother. He studied at Oxford, spent time in the military, and became a banker. After his bankruptcy, he was ordained. In 1797, Henry married Eliza de Feuillide (1761–1813), his glamorous older cousin. Eliza's first husband had been guillotined in 1794. Henry acted as Jane's agent and provided her with a base in London. He and Cassandra oversaw the publication of *Persuasion* and *Northanger Abbey* after Jane's death.

Cassandra (1773–1845) was Jane's only sister and her lifelong companion. She was engaged to a young clergyman, Thomas Fowle, but he died in 1797. Cassandra's sketch of Jane is the most reliably authenticated picture of her.

Francis or Frank (1774–1865) had a very successful naval career. He was eventually knighted and became Admiral of the Fleet. He had eleven children with his first wife, Mary Gibson, but she died in 1823. Five years later, he married Martha Lloyd, Jane's best friend, who was by then in her sixties.

Charles (1779–1852) also became an admiral. Jane's knowledge of and respect for the navy as seen in *Mansfield Park* and *Persuasion* stemmed from following her brothers' careers. Charles bought his sisters topaz crosses, the inspiration for Fanny Price's amber cross from her sailor brother, William. Charles married twice and had eight children, not all of whom survived.

Although most of their education took place at home, in 1783 Jane and Cassandra went away to boarding school in Oxford and then Southampton. Their cousin, Jane Cooper, went with them, and probably saved their lives by secretly writing to her mother when a typhoid epidemic broke out. The girls' mothers hurried to bring them home, but Mrs. Cooper contracted the disease and died. From 1785–86, Jane and Cassandra were boarders at The Abbey School in Reading. This may have been the model for Mrs. Goddard's School in *Emma*.

Jane catalogued her early literary efforts as *Volume the First*, *Volume the Second*, and *Volume the Third*. These early stories were often presented as (not particularly tactful) gifts to friends and relatives. They show Jane responding to her reading. The tone is often giggly, satirical, or burlesque (hungry children eat their mother's fingers, people fall over dead drunk) but her inimitable style is developing, particularly in *Catharine or The Bower*, written when she was just sixteen.

Jane's first "proper" novel was *Lady Susan*, begun in 1794, although not published until long after her death. It is a story of an older woman, a scheming seductress. After this, Jane went on to write *Elinor and Marianne* (later *Sense and Sensibility*) and then *First Impressions* (later *Pride and Prejudice*). In 1797, her father tried to interest the publishers Cadell and Davis in *First Impressions*, but they sent the manuscript back unopened. We haven't a record of Jane's reaction to this, so it's possible that she didn't even know her father had sent it in for consideration.

Jane's earliest surviving letter, from 1796, records her flirtation with Tom Lefroy. He was whisked away from Jane when his family got wind of the developing romance; she wasn't rich enough for the match to be deemed desirable.

In 1801, Mr. Austen retired and Jane, Cassandra, and their parents moved to Bath. The years there weren't very productive or happy, although the location was made useful in *Northanger Abbey* and *Persuasion*. In December 1802, Jane was staying with her friends Alethea and Catherine Bigg, when their awkward younger brother, Harris, asked her to marry him. Tempted by financial security, Jane accepted. The next day she realized she couldn't go through with it and she and Cassandra hurried away. Jane almost found love with a clergyman on a summer vacation in Sidmouth, but he died unexpectedly.

In 1803, Henry sold the manuscript of what was to become *Northanger Abbey* to the publishers Crosby & Co.; however, they sat on the novel and her career stalled again. She began *The Watsons*, but later abandoned it; perhaps it had become too depressing.

Mr. Austen died in January 1805. For a while after this, Jane, Cassandra, their mother, and Martha Lloyd lived together in a semi-nomadic way, renting houses and staying with relatives. Jane was happier in Southampton, where they shared a house with Frank's family. She finally found the tranquillity necessary for work after they moved to the cottage Edward gave them in Chawton in July 1809. *Sense and Sensibility* was published in 1811, and Jane's career took off. In 1813, she had real success with *Pride and Prejudice*.

During her Chawton years, Jane revised her earlier works, completed *Mansfield Park*, *Emma* and *Persuasion*, and started *Sanditon*. In 1816, Jane's health began to fail. In May 1817, to be near the best doctor, she and Cassandra moved to Winchester, but it was too late. On July 18th, at the age of forty-one, Jane died. She was buried in Winchester Cathedral.

BIBLIOGRAPHY

Austen, Caroline, *Reminiscences of Jane Austen's Niece,* introduced by Deirdre Le Faye (The Jane Austen Society, Chawton, 2004).

Austen, Jane, *Sense and Sensibility*; *Pride and Prejudice*; *Northanger Abbey*; *Mansfield Park*; *Emma*; *Persuasion*; *The Watsons*, *Lady Susan* and *Sanditon*; *Catharine and Other Writings* (Oxford University Press, The World's Classics editions, Oxford and Penguin English Library, Penguin Classics, and Penguin Popular Classics editions, London).

Austen-Leigh, James Edward, ed. Kathryn Sutherland, *A Memoir of Jane Austen and Other Family Recollections* (Oxford World Classics, Oxford, 2008).

Austen-Leigh, William and Austen-Leigh, Richard Arthur, *Jane Austen – A Family Record,* revised and enlarged by Deirdre Le Faye (The British Library, London, 1989).

Black, Maggie and Le Faye, Deirdre, *The Jane Austen Cookbook* (British Museum Press, London, 1995).

Boyle, Laura, *Cooking With Jane Austen and Friends* (Trail Publishing, Co Durham, 2010).

Burney, Fanny, *Camilla: Picture of Youth; Cecilia: or Memoirs of an Heiress; Evelina: or The History of A Young Lady's Entrance into the World* (Oxford University Press, The World's Classics Editions, Oxford, 2008. First published in 1782).

Day, Malcolm, *Voices From The World Of Jane Austen* (David and Charles, Newton Abbot, 2006).

Edgeworth, Maria *Belinda* (Oxford University Press, The World's Classics Editions, Oxford, 2008. First published in 1801).

Hannon, Patrice, *Dear Jane Austen: A Heroine's Guide to Life and Love* (Penguin, London, 2009).

Hardy, John, *Jane Austen's Heroines: Intimacy in Human Relationships* (Routledge, London, 1984).

Henderson, Lauren, *Jane Austen's Guide to Romance* (Headline Review, London, 2006).

Hill, Constance, *Jane Austen – Her Homes & Her Friends* (John Lane The Bodley Head, London, 1923. Also available from Elibron Classics Series).

Honan, Park *Jane Austen – Her Life* (Phoenix, Orion Books, London, 1997).

Le Faye, Deirdre, *Jane Austen's Letters* (Oxford University Press, Oxford, 1995).

Le Faye, Deirdre, *Jane Austen – The World of Her Novels* (Frances Lincoln Ltd, London, 2003).

Ray, Joan Klingel, *Jane Austen For Dummies* (Wiley Publishing Inc., Indianapolis, 2006).

Ross, Josephine and Webb, Henrietta (illus.), *Jane Austen's Guide to Good Manners* (Bloomsbury, London, 2009).

Shields, Carol, *Jane Austen* (Phoenix, Orion Books, London, 2001).

Sullivan, Margaret C., *The Jane Austen Handbook* (Quirk Books, Philadelphia, PA, 2007).

Tomalin, Claire, *Jane Austen – A Life* (Penguin, London, 2000).

Tucker, George Holbert, *A Goodly Heritage: A History of Jane Austen's Family* (Carcanet New Press, Manchester, 1983).

Wilson, Kim, *In The Garden With Jane Austen* (Frances Lincoln Ltd, London, 2009).

Wilson, Kim, *Tea with Jane Austen* (Frances Lincoln Ltd, London, 2011).

USEFUL WEBSITES

http://www.pemberley.com/janeinfo/brablets.html
Jane Austen's Letters. The text of the first (1884) edition of Jane Austen's *Letters* is available online

http://www.jane-austens-house-museum.org.uk/
Website of Jane Austen's House Museum in Chawton

http://www.janeausten.co.uk/
Website of The Jane Austen Centre, Bath

http://www.janeausten.ac.uk
A virtual collection of Jane Austen's manuscripts

http://www.pemberley.com/
The Republic of Pemberley website. Useful for texts of the novels, many letters, discussion, and information

http://austenonly.com/
An immensely useful and interesting blog

http://www.jasna.org/
Website of The Jane Austen Society of North America

http://www.janeaustensoci.freeuk.com
Website of The Jane Austen Society of the United Kingdom

ABBREVIATIONS

S&S	*Sense and Sensibility*
P&P	*Pride and Prejudice*
MP	*Mansfield Park*
E	*Emma*
NA	*Northanger Abbey*
P	*Persusasion*
W	*The Watsons*
S	*Sandition*

Footnotes: Chapter numbers assume a single modern volume for each novel rather than the original and more correct numbering which is still often used. The aim is to give readers new to Jane's work a better sense of where in the novel things occur. Either system works well. Electronic versions are easy to navigate too.

INDEX

ACKNOWLEDGMENTS

My heartfelt thanks go to the trustees, staff, and volunteers at Jane Austen's House Museum in Chawton for making me so welcome, and particularly Ann Channon, who so kindly read my manuscript; any mistakes are mine. I would also like to thank Arts Council England, who supported the residency. Jayne Ansell, Judith Chamberlain-Webber, and Viv Croot at Ivy Press have been endlessly enthusiastic and efficient. I am also very grateful to Wayne Blades and Glyn Bridgewater for their beautiful work on the design and illustrations. I would also like to thank my students at The University of Southampton, Viv and Jayne's friends at Ivy Press, my own dear mother, Shena Mackay, for coming up with ideas for the dilemmas, and Jen Eiss for helping to mold those ideas. My thanks also go to Sarah Lutyens and Anna Steadman at Lutyens and Rubinstein, and to Stephen Smith who has been as patient as Colonel Brandon.

PICTURE CREDITS